P9-CQM-578

cook's library
# One Pot

cook's library

# One Pot

*p*

This is a Parragon Publishing Book
This edition published in 2003

Parragon Publishing
Queen Street House
4 Queen Street
Bath BA1 1HE, UK

ISBN: 0-75259-952-6

Printed in China

**NOTE**

This book uses imperial and metric measurements. Follow the same
units of measurement throughout; do not mix imperial and metric.
All spoon measurements are level: teaspoons are assumed to be 5 ml,
and tablespoons are assumed to be 15 ml. Unless otherwise stated,
milk is assumed to be full fat, eggs and individual vegetables such as
potatoes are medium, and pepper is freshly ground black pepper.

The times given for each recipe are an approximate guide only because the
preparation times may differ according to the techniques used by different
people and the cooking times may vary as a result of the type of oven used.
The preparation times include chilling and marinating times, where appropriate.

Recipes using raw or very lightly cooked eggs should be
avoided by infants, the elderly, pregnant women, convalescents,
and anyone suffering from an illness.

# Contents

# Introduction

Cooking one-pot meals has many advantages, the most obvious of which is damage limitation—in other words, you don't have to spend time juggling numerous pans on your stove, only to follow an enjoyable meal with having to wash them all up. There are other, more subtle benefits, too. If there is only one pan to keep your eye on or, occasionally, when a second pan is required to prepare rice or pasta to accompany the one-pot meal—and many one-pot dishes require little attention during cooking anyway—there is less chance of something spoiling, boiling over or burning when your back is turned. Slow-cooked dishes in a casserole or covered pan lose fewer nutrients and the flavors of their ingredients are wonderfully enhanced and intermingled. At the opposite end of the spectrum, fast-cook, stir-fry dishes retain the color, texture, and flavor of their ingredients, plus much of their nutritional value. Last, but by no means least, using only one pot cuts down the amount of fuel required, assisting the family budget and the environment at the same time.

When you look through the collection of recipes in this book, you may be surprised to discover how versatile one-pot cooking is. Probably the first dishes that spring to mind are hearty and satisfying stews and there are certainly plenty of these, ranging from richly flavored Beef and Potato Goulash (see page 32) to spicy and exotic Thai Green Fish Curry (see page 154). These sorts of dishes are perfect for the busy cook with a hungry family, as once the initial preparation is completed, you can just leave the pot to bubble gently, emitting its appetizing aroma, while you get on with something else or even put your feet up for a while. Slow cooking is the best way with inexpensive cuts of meat, as its transforms them into melt-in-the-mouth tenderness, creating an economical, as well as delicious meal. As most stews taste even better on reheating, you can even prepare them the day before.

Lighter stews and meal-in-bowl soups are just made for those in-between occasions. When the weather lets you down and sunshine turns to miserable rain, what could be more cheering than a colorful Rich Chicken Casserole (see page 88)? Weekends are meant for relaxing, but, with a family, they often seem to be one long dash to complete the chores, do the shopping, and chauffeur the kids around. Solve the problem of Saturday lunch with a bowl of Tuscan Onion Soup (see page 96) or Fish and Crab Chowder (see page 142) and a loaf of fresh, crusty bread.

Pot roasts bring a welcome change to the family menu. They have all the advantages of a traditional roast—and are often much more succulent—with none of the bother and mess. As timing is not critical, they are also excellent for informal entertaining, allowing you to relax with your guests and not worry about late arrivals.

Bakes are always popular, whether family favorites, such as Macaroni Cheese and Tomato (see page 133), or more adventurous dishes, such as Seafood Lasagna (see page 164). As a rule, they cook more quickly than stews and casseroles, so they are a good choice for midweek suppers when less time is available.

Of course, when time is really short, reach for the wok. Stir-fried dishes are the original fast food. After all, the technique was invented to cope with a chronic fuel shortage—the ingredients all go into one pan and are cooked in minutes. Preparation takes a little longer, because it is important to make sure that everything is ready before you start cooking and that ingredients are chopped or sliced to about the same size so that they cook evenly. Even so, these are dishes that can take less than 10 minutes from kitchen to table. Pan-fried dishes are not usually quite so fast and, like stir-fries, do require quite a lot of attention during cooking. However, the results are worth it.

For those who love to cook, but can't stand washing dishes, the king of one-pot dishes must be the risotto, a glorious rice-based combination. For good results, you must use the highest quality ingredients—never leftovers—and you can't hurry a risotto. Once the rice starts cooking, you must stir assiduously and keep a sharp eye out for the precise moment to add more stock. The uniquely creamy result is worth the bother, whether delicate Minted Green Risotto (see page 112) or luxurious Rich Lobster Risotto (see page 171)— and you've still used only one pot. Other rice dishes, such as pilaus, may be less demanding, although no less delicious. While thinking about grains, don't overlook the ingenious Moroccan tagine. While a fabulous stew cooks in the pan below, couscous steams gently in a basket on top, so that they are ready to be served together.

# Equipment

Everything you require for satisfactory one-pot cooking is probably already in your kitchen, but if you are considering buying replacements or want to drop hints about gifts to family and friends, there are one or two things worth considering.

A set of good pans really is worth having. First, you do need a set because it is important to have the right size pan for the quantity of food you are cooking and this will vary depending on the particular recipe and the number of servings. The pan must be large enough to contain all the ingredients and to allow you stir them without sloshing them all over the stove, but not so big that the liquid evaporates and the food scorches or, worse, burns into a kind of welded mass on the base. Secondly, you need the best quality you can afford. Cheap, flimsy pans do not distribute the heat evenly, so look for those with a heavy base. A tight-fitting lid is essential and, if it is made of heatproof glass, you can check on progress without having to lift it. However, glass lids are more vulnerable to damage than metal ones—never run cold water straight on to a hot lid. If you have a dishwasher, make sure the pans are suitable. Some people prefer nonstick linings and modern ones are much more resilient than older linings. They are particularly useful if you are concerned about fat intake, as you can cook with less fat or oil than in a conventional pan.

Flameproof casseroles are one of humankind's greatest achievements. They can be used on the stove for softening onions and browning meat, then transferred straight to the oven or they can be used to cook the whole dish on the stove. Most of them are attractively designed, so they can also be transferred straight to the table without the need for extra serving dishes. Again, a range of sizes is useful.

A wok is also well worth having. It can be used for any number of cooking techniques in addition to stir-frying, including deep-frying and steaming. If you are going to buy only one, choose a wok that is bigger than you think you will need. They are available in a range of materials and, like pans, a heavy one is better than a flimsy one. Nonstick woks are available, but they cannot be heated to the high temperatures required for perfect stir-frying. Nonstick woks will almost certainly require seasoning

before use; follow the manufacturer's instructions. Some woks are sold with a dome-shaped lid, while others will require you to buy this separately. It is not essential, but is useful.

A heavy-based skillet is a worthwhile investment. Many professional cooks prefer cast-iron, although this will need seasoning, and heavy-gauge steel is also a good choice. A skillet with a metal handle can also be used under the broiler to brown the tops of dishes, such as frittata. However, this can be a safety hazard for careless cooks, so if you fall into this category, make sure you have a well-secured wooden handle (you can always cover it in foil to put it under the broiler). Whether the pan has a nonstick lining is a matter of personal choice.

In a strict definition of one-pot cooking, steamers could be seen as cheating, but they are invaluable. Extra vegetables, grains, or even desserts can be steamed above the main dish, using no extra fuel and creating very little more dish-washing. Chinese stacking bamboo steamers are inexpensive and easy to use with a wok, while collapsible metal ones are convenient if your storage space is limited.

Preparation is an integral part of cooking and, again, time and effort are saved if you have the right tools. Sharp knives are essential, because they speed up slicing and chopping, ensure even-size and neatly shaped pieces and are safer—it's the blunt knives that slip and cut fingers. You will need a minimum of two. A cook's knife is used for chopping or slicing vegetables, herbs, and meat. Choose one with a heavy, wide blade, about 7–8 inches/18–20 cm long. A small paring knife, about $3\frac{1}{4}$–4 inches/8–10 cm long, is the best size for peeling and trimming vegetables. There are many other sorts of knives—bread, utility, cheese, grapefruit, ham, and tomato, for example—and the bigger the selection you have, the more likely you will be able to match the right tool to the job.

A swivel-blade vegetable peeler is inexpensive and easier to use than a knife. As the nutrients in many vegetables, such as potatoes, are concentrated directly beneath the skin, peeling them thinly makes sense. You can also use a vegetable peeler for shaving Parmesan or other hard cheese for garnishes.

Cutting boards are necessary and you should use separate boards for raw meat, poultry, and fish and for vegetables to avoid cross contamination. Materials vary from wood to plastic and even glass and all have both advantages and disadvantages. Traditional wooden blocks, at least $1\frac{1}{2}$ inches/4 cm thick, are the most popular and practical,

but they cannot be sterilized. Plastic boards are less appealing, but can be bleached or washed with boiling water and are dishwasher safe. Laminated cutting boards are best kept for decoration, because they are dangerously slippery and, given that the laminate chips easily and lifts with time, they may be unhygienic.

Measuring spoons and cups and kitchen scales take the guesswork out of cooking. However, precise measurements are not usually so critical with one-pot cooking as they are with, say, baking. In all recipes, spoon measurements are level, rather than heaping.

There are, of course, masses of other kitchen tools and all have their uses—some more frequently than others. Small items, such as a can opener, draining and wooden spoons and a lemon squeezer or reamer, can be acquired over time. Larger, more expensive equipment, such as a food processor, make life easier, but they are a major investment. If you don't have one, don't despair—a box grater is adequate for cheese and bread crumbs, you can push a mixture through a wire strainer to purée it and a heavy mortar and pestle is just as good for grinding. As with equipment for any activity, from carpentry to cooking, whatever you are buying, it is worth paying for the best quality that you can afford.

# Little Extras

All the recipes in this book are designed to stand alone as an adequate, tasty, and nutritious meal, but with little extra effort or cost, you can turn an ordinary supper into a special occasion. A judicious use of ready-prepared accompaniments and garnishes also makes entertaining easy.

Nowadays, supermarket shelves are stacked with a marvelous selection of breads and rolls, from the ever-popular French baguette to Italian focaccia and ciabatta and from Indian nan to Lebanese flatbreads. Serve them with risottos, curries, and bakes, as well as soups and stews. Packs of prepared mixed salad greens make an easy and refreshing accompaniment to almost any dish. You don't even have to make your own dressing, as a vast range, from thousand island to simple vinaigrette, is on sale. Pasta salads, coleslaw, tabbouleh, and many other salads can be found on the delicatessen counter in the supermarket, where you can also buy olives, gherkins, and other pickles.

Many of the recipes suggest a suitable garnish, and almost every dish looks more attractive sprinkled with chopped fresh herbs. Other easy garnishes include chopped nuts and seeds. Ready-made croûtons are an inexpensive and useful pantry item.

When you are shopping, it is worth keeping your eyes open for these little extras that will give your one-pot meals that finishing touch.

# Basic Recipes

These recipes form the basis of several of the dishes contained throughout this book. Many of these basic recipes can be made in advance and stored in the refrigerator until required.

## Fresh Chicken Bouillon

MAKES

7 cups

2 lb 4 oz/1 kg chicken, skinned
2 celery stalks, chopped
1 onion, sliced
2 carrots, chopped
1 garlic clove
few sprigs of fresh parsley
8 cups water
salt and pepper

1 Place all the ingredients in a large pan and bring to a boil.

2 Skim away any surface froth using a large flat spoon. Reduce the heat to a gentle simmer, partially cover, and cook for 2 hours. Let cool.

3 Line a strainer with clean cheesecloth and place over a large pitcher or bowl. Pour the bouillon through the strainer. The cooked chicken can be used in another recipe. Discard the other solids. Cover the bouillon and chill.

4 Skim off surface fat before using. Store in the refrigerator for up to 3 days, or freeze in small batches until required.

## Fresh Vegetable Bouillon

MAKES

7 cups

1 large onion, sliced
1 large carrot, diced
1 celery stalk, chopped
2 garlic cloves
1 dried bay leaf
few sprigs of fresh parsley
pinch of grated nutmeg
8 cups water
salt and pepper

1 Place all the ingredients in a large pan and bring to a boil.

2 Skim away any surface froth using a large flat spoon. Reduce the heat to a gentle simmer, partially cover, and cook for 45 minutes. Let cool.

3 Line a strainer with clean cheesecloth and place over a large pitcher or bowl. Pour the bouillon through the strainer. Discard the solids.

4 Cover the bouillon and store in the refrigerator for up to 3 days, or freeze in small portions.

## Fresh Fish Bouillon

MAKES

7 cups

2 lb 4 oz/1 kg white fish bones, heads, and scraps
1 large onion, chopped
2 carrots, chopped
2 celery stalks, chopped
½ tsp black peppercorns
½ tsp grated lemon rind
few sprigs of fresh parsley
8 cups water
salt and pepper

1 Rinse the fish trimmings in cold water and place in a large pan with the other ingredients. Bring to the boil.

2 Skim away any surface froth using a large flat spoon.

3 Reduce the heat to a gentle simmer and cook, partially covered, for 30 minutes. Let cool.

4 Line a strainer with clean cheesecloth and place over a large pitcher or bowl. Pour the bouillon through the strainer. Discard the solids. Cover the bouillon and store in the refrigerator for up to 3 days until required, or freeze in small batches.

# Fresh Beef Bouillon

**MAKES**
7 cups

about 2 lb 4 oz/1 kg bones from a cooked joint or raw chopped beef
2 onions, studded with 6 cloves, or sliced or chopped coarsely
2 carrots, sliced
1 leek, sliced
1–2 celery stalks, sliced
1 Bouquet Garni
9½ cups water

1 Use chopped marrow bones with a few strips of shin of beef, if possible. Put in a roasting pan and cook in a preheated oven, 450°F/230°C, for 30–50 minutes, until browned.

2 Transfer to a large pan with the other ingredients. Bring to a boil and remove any froth from the surface.

3 Cover and simmer gently for 3–4 hours. Strain the bouillon and let cool. Remove any fat from the surface and chill. If stored for more than 24 hours the bouillon must be boiled every day, cooled quickly, and chilled again.

4 The bouillon may be frozen for up to 2 months: place in a large plastic bag and seal, leaving at least 1 inch/2.5 cm of headspace to allow for expansion.

# Chinese Bouillon

**MAKES**
10 cups

1 lb 10 oz/750 g chicken pieces, trimmed and chopped
1 lb 10 oz/750 g pork spare ribs
15 cups cold water
3–4 pieces of fresh gingerroot, chopped
3–4 scallions, each tied into a knot
3–4 tbsp Chinese rice wine or dry sherry

1 Place the chicken and pork in a large pan with the water. Add the ginger and scallions.

2 Bring to a boil, and skim away any surface froth using a large flat spoon. Reduce the heat and simmer, uncovered, for at least 2–3 hours.

3 Strain the bouillon, discarding the chicken, pork, gingerroot, and scallions. Add the Chinese rice wine and return to a boil, then reduce the heat and simmer for 2–3 minutes. Let cool.

4 Refrigerate the bouillon when cool, it will keep for up to 4–5 days. Alternatively, it can be frozen in small batches and defrosted as required.

# Cornstarch Paste

Mix 1 part cornstarch with about 1.5 parts of cold water. Stir until smooth. The paste can be used to thicken sauces.

# Fresh Bouquet Garni

1 fresh or dried bay leaf
few sprigs of fresh parsley
few sprigs of fresh thyme

Tie the herbs together with a length of string or cotton.

# Dried Bouquet Garni

1 dried bay leaf
good pinch of dried mixed herbs or any one herb
good pinch of dried parsley
8–10 black peppercorns
2–4 cloves
1 garlic clove (optional)

Put all the ingredients in a small square of cheesecloth and secure with string or cotton, leaving a long tail so it can be tied to the handle of the pan for easy removal.

# How to Use This Book

Each recipe contains a wealth of useful information, including a breakdown of nutritional quantities, preparation, and cooking times, and level of difficulty. All of this information is explained in detail below.

A full-color photograph of the finished dish.

The ingredients for each recipe are listed in the order that they are used.

The nutritional information provided for each recipe is per serving or per portion. Optional ingredients, variations or serving suggestions have not been included in the calculations.

The method is clearly explained with step-by-step instructions that are easy to follow.

Cook's tips provide useful information regarding ingredients or cooking techniques.

⭐ The number of stars represents the difficulty of each recipe, ranging from very easy (1 star) to challenging (4 stars).

This amount of time represents the preparation of ingredients, including cooling, chilling, and soaking times.

🕐 This represents the cooking time.

# Meat

From ham to sausages and from beef to pork, you are sure to find an easy-to-prepare midweek supper or something special to serve guests. This chapter is packed with great ideas for meaty soups, succulent stews, spicy curries, and almost instant stir-fries. It includes familiar favorites, such as Scotch Broth (see page 20) and Chili con Carne (see page 33), and classic dishes, such as Pork Stroganoff (see page 40) and Lamb Biryani (see page 49). Adventurous cooks will enjoy experimenting with more unusual meats, trying out such recipes as Sweet & Sour Venison Stir-Fry (see page 50). There are meals with child appeal, luxurious special occasion dishes, hearty winter-warmers, tasty light lunches, hot or aromatic curries, and recipes from countries as far apart as China, Mexico, and Italy, In fact, something to suit all tastes—just popped into the pot.

This traditional winter soup is full of goodness, with lots of tasty golden vegetables along with tender barley and lamb.

# Scotch Broth

**SERVES 4 – 6**

¼ cup pearl barley
10½ oz/300 g lean boneless lamb, such as shoulder fillet, trimmed of fat and cut into ½-inch/1-cm cubes
3 cups water
2 garlic cloves, chopped finely or crushed
4 cups chicken or meat bouillon
1 onion, chopped finely
1 bay leaf
1 large leek, quartered lengthwise and sliced
2 large carrots, diced finely
1 parsnip, diced finely
1 cup diced rutabaga
2 tbsp chopped fresh parsley
salt and pepper

1 Rinse the barley under cold running water. Put in a pan and add water to cover generously. Bring to a boil over medium heat and boil for 3 minutes, skimming off the foam from the surface. Remove the pan from the heat, cover, and set aside.

2 Put the lamb in another large pan with the measured water and bring to a boil. Skim off the foam that rises to the surface.

3 Stir in the garlic, bouillon, onion, and bay leaf. Reduce the heat, partially cover, and simmer for 15 minutes.

4 Drain the barley and add to the soup. Add the leek, carrots, parsnip, and rutabaga. Simmer, stirring occasionally, for about 1 hour or until the lamb and vegetables are tender.

5 Season to taste with salt and pepper, stir in the parsley, and serve.

**NUTRITION**
Calories *186*; Sugars *6 g*; Protein *13 g*; Carbohydrate *23 g*; Fat *5 g*; Saturates *2 g*

 moderate

 10–15 mins

 1 hr 30 mins

 **COOK'S TIP**

This soup is lean when the lamb is trimmed. By making it beforehand and chilling in the refrigerator, you can remove any hardened fat before reheating.

Packed with tomatoes, garbanzo beans, and vegetables, this thick and hearty entrée soup is bursting with exotic flavors and aromas.

# Spicy Lamb Soup

1 Heat the oil in a large pan or flameproof casserole over medium-high heat. Add the lamb, in batches if necessary, and cook, stirring occasionally, until evenly browned on all sides, adding a little more oil if needed. Remove the meat, with a draining spoon.

2 Reduce the heat and add the onion and garlic to the pan. Cook, stirring frequently, for 1–2 minutes.

3 Add the water and return all the meat to the pan. Bring just to a boil and skim off any foam that rises to the surface. Reduce the heat and stir in the tomatoes, bay leaf, thyme, oregano, cinnamon, cumin, turmeric, and harissa. Simmer for about 1 hour or until the meat is tender. Discard the bay leaf.

4 Stir in the garbanzo beans, carrot, and potato and simmer for about 15 minutes. Add the zucchini and peas and simmer for another 15–20 minutes or until all the vegetables are tender.

5 Season to taste with salt and pepper and add more harissa if desired. Ladle the soup into warmed bowls, garnish with chopped fresh mint or cilantro, and serve immediately.

## SERVES 4

1–2 tbsp olive oil
1 lb/450 g lean boneless lamb, such as shoulder fillet, trimmed of fat and cut into ½-inch/1-cm cubes
1 onion, chopped finely
2–3 garlic cloves, crushed
5 cups water
14 oz/400 g canned chopped tomatoes
1 bay leaf
½ tsp dried thyme
½ tsp dried oregano
pinch of ground cinnamon
¼ tsp ground cumin
¼ tsp ground turmeric
1 tsp harissa
14 oz/400 g canned garbanzo beans, drained
1 carrot, diced
1 potato, diced
1 zucchini, quartered lengthwise and sliced
1 cup fresh or thawed frozen green peas
salt and pepper
chopped fresh mint or cilantro leaves, to garnish

## NUTRITION
Calories 323; Sugars 6 g; Protein 27 g; Carbohydrate 25 g; Fat 13 g; Saturates 4 g

 moderate

10 mins

1 hr 45 mins

Strips of tender lean beef are combined with crisp water chestnuts and cooked rice in a tasty beef broth with a tang of orange.

# Beef, Water Chestnut, *and* Rice Soup

**SERVES 4**

12 oz/350 g lean beef (such as round or sirloin)
4 cups Fresh Beef Bouillon (see page 15)
cinnamon stick, broken
2 star anise
2 tbsp dark soy sauce
2 tbsp dry sherry
3 tbsp tomato paste
4 oz/115 g canned water chestnuts, drained and sliced
3 cups cooked white rice
1 tsp grated orange rind
6 tbsp orange juice
salt and pepper

*to garnish*
strips of orange rind
2 tbsp chopped chives

1  Carefully trim away any fat from the beef. Cut the beef into thin strips and then place into a large saucepan.

2  Pour over the bouillon and add the cinnamon, star anise, soy sauce, sherry, tomato paste, and water chestnuts. Bring to a boil, skimming away any surface froth with a flat ladle or draining spoon. Cover the pan and simmer gently for about 20 minutes or until the beef is tender.

3  Skim the soup to remove any froth again. Remove and discard the cinnamon and star anise and blot the surface with paper towels to remove any fat.

4  Stir in the rice, orange rind, and juice. Adjust the seasoning if necessary. Heat through for 2–3 minutes before ladling into warm bowls. Serve garnished with strips of orange rind and chopped chives.

**NUTRITION**
Calories *219*; Sugars *5 g*; Protein *27 g*;
Carbohydrate *20 g*; Fat *8 g*; Saturates *2 g*

 easy

15 mins

25 mins

**COOK'S TIP**

Omit the rice for a lighter soup that is an ideal starter for an Asian meal of many courses. For a more substantial soup that would be a meal in its own right, add diced vegetables such as carrot, bell pepper, corn, or zucchini.

A wonderful meal-in-a-bowl, this soup is ideal for a winter supper or lunch. The beefy flavor, enhanced with spices, is very warming.

# Beef *and* Vegetable Soup

1 To peel the tomatoes, place them in a heatproof bowl, pour in enough boiling water to cover, and let stand for 30 seconds. Drain and plunge into cold water. The skins will then slide off easily. Chop the tomatoes.

2 Using a large knife, cut the corn cobs into 1-inch/2.5-cm pieces.

3 Place the bouillon in a pan with the tomatoes, carrot, onion, potatoes, and cabbage. Bring to a boil, then reduce the heat and simmer for 10–15 minutes or until the vegetables are tender.

4 Add the corn cob pieces, the cumin, chili powder, paprika, and beef pieces. Bring back to a boil over medium heat and cook until heated through.

5 Ladle into warmed soup bowls and serve sprinkled with fresh cilantro, if using, with a salsa of your choice handed around separately.

**SERVES 4 – 6**

3 medium tomatoes
2 corn cobs
4 cups beef bouillon
1 carrot, sliced thinly
1 onion, chopped
1–2 small potatoes, diced
¼ cabbage, sliced thinly
¼ tsp ground cumin
¼ tsp mild chili powder
¼ tsp paprika
8 oz/225 g cooked beef, cut into bite-size pieces
3–4 tbsp chopped fresh cilantro (optional)
hot salsa of your choice, to serve

**NUTRITION**
Calories *167*; Sugars *7 g*; Protein *16 g*; Carbohydrate *17 g*; Fat *5 g*; Saturates *2 g*

 easy
15 mins
20 mins

🍳 **COOK'S TIP**

To give the soup it a flavor of tamaile, the popular Mexican steamed dumplings, add a few tablespoons of masa harina, mixed into a thinnish paste with a little water, at Step 4. Stir well, then continue cooking until thickened.

Veal plays an important role in Italian cuisine and there are dozens of recipes for all cuts of this meat.

# Tuscan Veal Broth

**SERVES 4**

$^1\!/_3$ cup dried peas, soaked for 2 hours
  and drained
2 lb/900 g boned neck of veal, diced
5 cups Fresh Beef or Bouillon (see page 15)
$2^1\!/_4$ cups water
$^1\!/_3$ cup pearl barley, washed
1 large carrot, diced
1 small turnip (about 6 oz/175 g), diced
1 large leek, sliced thinly
1 red onion, chopped finely
$^1\!/_2$ cup chopped tomatoes
1 sprig of fresh basil
$^3\!/_4$ cup dried vermicelli
salt and white pepper

1 Put the peas, veal, bouillon, and water into a large saucepan and bring to a boil over a low heat. Using a draining spoon, skim off any froth that rises to the surface of the liquid.

2 When all of the froth has been removed, add the pearl barley and a pinch of salt to the mixture. Simmer gently over low heat for 25 minutes.

3 Add the carrot, turnip, leek, onion, tomatoes, and basil to the pan, and season with salt and pepper to taste. Let simmer for about 2 hours, skimming the surface, using a draining spoon, from time to time. Remove the pan from the heat and set aside for 2 hours.

4 Set the pan over a medium heat and bring to a boil. Add the vermicelli and cook for 12 minutes. Season with salt and pepper to taste and remove and discard the basil. Ladle into soup bowls and serve immediately.

**NUTRITION**
Calories *420*; Sugars *5 g*; Protein *54 g*;
Carbohydrate *37 g*; Fat *7 g*; Saturates *2 g*

 challenging

2 hrs 15 mins

4 hrs 45 mins

Wild mushrooms are available commercially and an increasing range of cultivated varieties is now to be found in many supermarkets.

# Veal *and* Wild Mushroom Soup

1 Put the veal, bones, and water into a large saucepan. Bring to a boil and lower the heat. Add the onion, peppercorns, cloves, and mace and simmer for about 3 hours, until the veal bouillon is reduced by one third.

2 Strain the bouillon, skim off any fat on the surface with a draining spoon, and pour the bouillon into a clean saucepan. Add the veal meat to the pan.

3 Add the mushrooms and cream, bring to a boil over low heat and then let simmer for 12 minutes, stirring occasionally.

4 Meanwhile, cook the vermicelli in lightly salted boiling water for 10 minutes or until tender, but still firm to the bite. Drain and keep warm.

5 Mix the cornstarch and milk to form a smooth paste. Stir into the soup to thicken. Season to taste with salt and pepper and just before serving, add the vermicelli. Transfer the soup to a warm tureen and serve immediately.

### SERVES 4

1 lb/450 g veal, sliced thinly
1 lb/450 g veal bones
5 cups water
1 small onion
6 peppercorns
1 tsp cloves
pinch of mace
5 oz/140 g oyster and shiitake mushrooms, chopped coarsely
2/3 cup heavy cream
3/4 cup dried vermicelli
1 tbsp cornstarch
3 tbsp milk
salt and pepper

### NUTRITION

Calories *413*; Sugars *3 g*; Protein *28 g*; Carbohydrate *28 g*; Fat *22 g*; Saturates *12 g*

easy

5 mins

3 hrs 15 mins

### 🍳 COOK'S TIP

You can make this soup with the more inexpensive cuts of veal, such as breast or neck slices. The long cooking time ensures that the meat is really tender.

Spicy or smoky sausages add substance to this soup, which makes a hearty and warming supper, served with crusty bread and green salad.

# Cabbage Soup *with* Sausage

### SERVES 6

12 oz/350 g lean sausages, preferably highly seasoned
2 tsp oil
1 onion, chopped finely
1 leek, halved lengthwise and sliced thinly
2 carrots, halved and sliced thinly
400 g/14 oz canned chopped tomatoes
4 cups cored and coarsely shredded young green cabbage
1–2 garlic cloves, chopped finely
pinch of dried thyme
6¼ cups chicken or meat bouillon
salt and pepper
freshly grated Parmesan cheese, to serve

1 Put the sausages in water to cover generously and bring to a boil. Reduce the heat and simmer until firm. Drain the sausages and, when cool enough to handle, remove the skin, if you wish, and slice thinly.

2 Heat the oil in a large saucepan over medium heat, add the onion, leek, and carrots and cook for 3–4 minutes, stirring frequently, until the onion starts to soften.

3 Add the tomatoes, cabbage, garlic, thyme, bouillon, and sausages. Bring to a boil, reduce the heat to low and cook gently, partially covered, for about 40 minutes until the vegetables are tender.

4 Taste the soup and adjust the seasoning, if necessary. Ladle into warm bowls and serve with Parmesan cheese.

### NUTRITION
Calories 246; Sugars 13 g; Protein 15 g; Carbohydrate 21 g; Fat 12 g; Saturates 4 g

easy

15 mins

1 hr 5 mins

### 🍳 COOK'S TIP

If you don't have fresh bouillon available, use water instead, with 1 bouillon cube only dissolved in it. Add a little more onion and garlic, plus a bouquet garni (remove it before serving).

This meaty chili soup tastes lighter than one made with beef. Good for informal entertaining, the recipe is easily doubled.

# Pork Chili Soup

1 Heat the oil in a pan over medium-high heat. Add the pork, season with salt and pepper, and cook, stirring frequently, until no longer pink. Reduce the heat to medium and add the onion, celery, bell pepper, and garlic. Cover and cook, stirring occasionally, for a further 5 minutes until the onion is softened.

2 Add the tomatoes, tomato paste, and the bouillon. Stir in the coriander, cumin, oregano, and chili powder. Season with salt and pepper to taste.

3 Bring just to a boil, then reduce the heat to low, cover, and simmer for about 30–40 minutes until all the vegetables are very tender. Taste and adjust the seasoning, adding more chili powder if you like it hotter.

4 Ladle the chili into warm bowls and sprinkle with chopped cilantro or parsley. You can either hand the sour cream separately or top each serving with a spoonful.

**SERVES 3**

2 tsp olive oil
1 lb/450 g lean ground pork
1 onion, chopped finely
1 celery stalk, chopped finely
1 bell pepper, seeded and chopped finely
2–3 garlic cloves, chopped finely
14 oz/400 g canned chopped tomatoes in juice
3 tbsp tomato paste
2 cups chicken or meat bouillon
¼ tsp ground coriander
¼ tsp ground cumin
¼ tsp dried oregano
1 tsp mild chili powder
salt and pepper
chopped fresh cilantro leaves or parsley, to garnish
sour cream, to serve

**NUTRITION**
Calories 308; Sugars 13 g; Protein 40 g; Carbohydrate 15 g; Fat 10 g; Saturates 3 g

 easy

10 mins

50–60 mins

Prosciutto is a cured ham, which is air- and salt-dried for up to 1 year. Parma ham is said to be the best of the many different varieties available.

# Garbanzo Beans *and* Prosciutto

### SERVES 4

1 tbsp olive oil
1 medium onion, sliced thinly
1 garlic clove, chopped
1 small red bell pepper, seeded and cut into thin strips
7 oz/200 g prosciutto, diced
14 oz/400 g canned garbanzo beans, drained and rinsed
1 tbsp chopped fresh parsley, to garnish
crusty bread, to serve

1 Heat the oil in a skillet. Add the onion, garlic, and bell pepper and cook over medium heat, stirring occasionally, for 3–4 minutes or until the vegetables have softened. Add the prosciutto and cook for 5 minutes or until the ham is just beginning to brown.

2 Add the garbanzo beans to the skillet and cook, stirring constantly, for 2–3 minutes until warmed through.

3 Sprinkle with chopped parsley and transfer to warm serving plates. Serve with lots of fresh crusty bread.

### NUTRITION
Calories *180*; Sugars *2 g*; Protein *12 g*;
Carbohydrate *18 g*; Fat *7 g*; Saturates *1 g*

⭐⭐⭐    moderate

🕐    10 mins

🕐    15 mins

### 🍴 COOK'S TIP

Whenever possible, use fresh herbs. They are becoming more readily available, and you can now buy small pots of herbs from the supermarket or grocery store and grow them at home.

If you can get fresh peas—and willing helpers to shell them—do use them: you will need 2 lb/1 kg. Add them to the pan with the bouillon.

# Rice *and* Peas

1 Heat the olive oil and half of the butter in a heavy pan. Add the pancetta or bacon and onion and cook over low heat, stirring occasionally, for 5 minutes until the onion is softened and translucent, but not browned.

2 Add the bouillon and fresh peas, if using, to the pan and bring to a boil. Stir in the rice and season to taste with pepper. Bring to a boil, lower the heat, and simmer, stirring occasionally, for 20–30 minutes until the rice is tender.

3 Add the parsley and frozen or canned baby peas, if using these instead of fresh peas, and cook for about 8 minutes until the peas are heated through. Stir in the remaining butter and the Parmesan.

4 Transfer to a warmed serving dish and serve immediately with freshly ground black pepper.

**SERVES  4**

1 tbsp olive oil
4 tbsp butter
2 oz/55 g pancetta or fatty bacon, chopped
1 small onion, chopped
6¼ cups hot chicken bouillon
1 cup risotto rice
3 tbsp chopped fresh parsley
2 cups fresh, frozen or canned baby peas
½ cup freshly grated Parmesan cheese
pepper

**NUTRITION**
Calories *409*; Sugars *2 g*; Protein *15 g*;
Carbohydrate *38 g*; Fat *23 g*; Saturates *12 g*

  easy

  10 mins

  50 mins

A filling and satisfying bake of lean ground beef, zucchini, and tomatoes, cooked in a low-fat "custard" with a cheese crust.

# Beef *and* Tomato Gratin

**SERVES  4**

12 oz/350 g lean ground beef
1 large onion, chopped finely
1 tsp dried mixed herbs
1 tbsp all-purpose flour
1¼ cups beef bouillon
1 tbsp tomato paste
2 large tomatoes, sliced thinly
4 zucchini, sliced thinly
2 tbsp cornstarch
1¼ cups skim milk
¾ cup ricotta cheese
1 egg yolk
scant ¾ cup freshly grated Parmesan cheese
salt and pepper

*to serve*
crusty bread
steamed vegetables

1 In a large skillet, dry-cook the beef and onion over low heat, stirring occasionally, for 4–5 minutes until the meat is browned.

2 Stir in the dried mixed herbs, flour, beef bouillon, and tomato paste, and season to taste with salt and pepper. Bring to a boil and simmer gently for 30 minutes until the mixture has thickened.

3 Transfer the beef mixture to an ovenproof gratin dish. Cover with a layer of sliced tomatoes and then add a layer of sliced zucchini. Blend the cornstarch with a little milk to a smooth paste. Pour the remaining milk into a pan and bring to a boil. Add the cornstarch mixture and cook, stirring constantly, for 1–2 minutes until thickened. Remove the pan from the heat and beat in the ricotta cheese and egg yolk. Season well with salt and pepper.

4 Spread the white sauce over the layer of zucchini. Place the dish on a cookie sheet and sprinkle the grated Parmesan cheese evenly over the top. Bake in a preheated oven, 375°F/190°C, for 25–30 minutes until golden brown. Serve with crusty bread and vegetables.

**NUTRITION**
Calories *278*; Sugars *10 g*; Protein *29 g*;
Carbohydrate *20 g*; Fat *10 g*; Saturates *5 g*

  moderate
10 mins
1 hr 15 mins

This rich, smoky-flavored Mexican stew is delicious; leftovers make a great filling for tacos, too.

# Michoacan Beef

1 Place the flour in a large bowl and season with salt and pepper. Add the beef and toss to coat well. Remove from the bowl, shaking off the excess flour.

2 Heat the oil in a skillet and brown the meat briefly over high heat. Reduce the heat to medium, add the onions and garlic, and cook for 2 minutes.

3 Add the tomatoes, chiles, pinch of sugar, and bouillon, cover, and simmer over low heat for 1½ hours or until the meat is very tender, adding the green beans 15 minutes before the end of the cooking time. Skim off any fat that rises to the surface.

4 Transfer to individual bowls and serve with simmered beans and rice.

**SERVES 4 – 6**

about 3 tbsp all-purpose flour
2 lb 4 oz/1 kg stewing beef, cut into large bite-size pieces
2 tbsp vegetable oil
2 onions, chopped
5 garlic cloves, chopped
4–5 medium tomatoes, diced
1½ dried chipotle chiles, reconstituted, seeded, and cut into thin strips, or a few shakes of bottled chipotle salsa
6¼ cups beef bouillon
3 cups green beans
pinch of sugar
salt and pepper

*to serve*
simmered beans
cooked rice

**NUTRITION**
Calories *315*; Sugars *6 g*; Protein *41 g*;
Carbohydrate *16 g*; Fat *10 g*; Saturates *3 g*

⭐⭐ easy
🕐 10 mins
🕐 2 hrs

🧑‍🍳 **COOK'S TIP**

This is traditionally made with nopales, edible cacti, which give the dish a distinctive flavor. Look for them in specialist stores. For this recipe you need 12–14 oz/350– 400 g canned or fresh nopales.

In this recipe, the potatoes are actually cooked in the goulash. For a change, you may prefer to substitute small, scrubbed new potatoes.

# Beef *and* Potato Goulash

## SERVES 4

2 tbsp vegetable oil
1 large onion, sliced
2 garlic cloves, crushed
1 lb 10 oz/750 g lean stewing steak
2 tbsp paprika
14 oz/400 g canned chopped tomatoes
2 tbsp tomato paste
1 large red bell pepper, seeded and chopped
3 cups sliced mushrooms
2½ cups beef bouillon
1 lb/450 g potatoes, cut into large chunks
1 tbsp cornstarch
salt and pepper

*to garnish*
4 tbsp low-fat plain yogurt
paprika
chopped fresh parsley

1 Heat the oil in a large pan. Add the onion and garlic and cook over medium heat, stirring occasionally, for 3–4 minutes until softened.

2 Cut the steak into chunks, add to the pan, and cook over high heat for about 3 minutes until browned all over.

3 Lower the heat to medium and stir in the paprika. Add the tomatoes, tomato paste, bell pepper,. and mushrooms. Cook, stirring, for 2 minutes.

4 Pour in the beef bouillon. Bring to a boil, stirring occasionally, then reduce the heat to low. Cover and simmer gently for about 1½ hours until the meat is cooked through and tender.

5 Add the potatoes, cover, and cook for another 20–30 minutes until tender.

6 Blend the cornstarch with a little water and add to the pan, stirring until thickened and blended. Cook for 1 minute, then season with salt and pepper to taste. Top with the yogurt, sprinkle over the paprika and chopped fresh parsley, and serve immediately.

## NUTRITION

Calories *477*; Sugars *11 g*; Protein *47 g*; Carbohydrate *39 g*; Fat *16 g*; Saturates *5 g*

 easy

15 mins

 2 hrs 15 mins

Probably the best known Mexican dish and one that is a great favorite with all. The chili content can be increased to taste.

# Chili *con* Carne

1 Cut the beef into ¾-inch/2-cm cubes. Heat the oil in a flameproof casserole and fry the beef until well sealed. Remove from the casserole.

2 Add the onion and garlic to the casserole and cook until lightly browned. Stir in the flour and cook for 1–2 minutes. Stir in the tomato juice and tomatoes and bring to a boil. Replace the beef and add the chili sauce, cumin, and seasoning. Cover and place in a preheated oven, 325°F/160°C, for 1½ hours or until almost tender.

3 Stir in the beans, oregano, and parsley and adjust the seasoning. Cover the casserole and return to the oven for 45 minutes. Serve sprinkled with herbs and with boiled rice and tortillas.

**SERVES 4**

1 lb 10 oz/785 g lean braising or stewing steak
2 tbsp vegetable oil
1 large onion, sliced
2–4 garlic cloves, crushed
1 tbsp all-purpose flour
scant 2 cups tomato juice
14 oz/400 g canned tomatoes
1–2 tbsp sweet chili sauce
1 tsp ground cumin
15 oz/425 g canned red kidney beans, drained
½ teaspoon dried oregano
1–2 tbsp chopped fresh parsley
salt and pepper
chopped fresh herbs, to garnish
boiled rice and tortillas, to serve

**NUTRITION**
Calories *443*; Sugars *11 g*; Protein *48 g*; Carbohydrate *30 g*; Fat *15 g*; Saturates *4 g*

 easy

5 mins

2 hrs 30 mins

 **COOK'S TIP**

Because chili con carne requires quite a lengthy cooking time, it saves time and fuel to prepare double the quantity you need and freeze half of it to serve on another occasion. Thaw and use within 3–4 weeks.

The spicy peanut sauce in this recipe will complement almost any meat; the dish is just as delicious made with chicken or pork.

# Potato, Beef, *and* Peanut Pot

**SERVES 4**

1 tbsp vegetable oil
5 tbsp butter
1 lb/450 g lean steak, cut into thin strips
1 onion, halved and sliced
2 garlic cloves, crushed
1 lb 5 oz/560 g potatoes, cubed
½ tsp paprika
4 tbsp crunchy peanut butter
2½ cups beef bouillon
4 tbsp unsalted peanuts
2 tsp light soy sauce
¾ cup sugar snap peas
1 red bell pepper, seeded and sliced
sprigs of fresh parsley, to garnish (optional)

1 Heat the oil and butter in a flameproof casserole.

2 Add the steak strips and cook them gently for about 3–4 minutes, stirring and turning the meat until it is sealed on all sides.

3 Add the onion and garlic to the meat and cook for a further 2 minutes, stirring constantly.

4 Add the potato cubes and cook for 3–4 minutes or until they begin to brown.

5 Stir in the paprika and peanut butter, then gradually stir in the beef bouillon. Bring the mixture to a boil, stirring frequently.

6 Finally, add the peanuts, soy sauce, sugar snap peas, and red bell pepper.

7 Cover the casserole and cook over low heat for 45 minutes or until the beef is cooked right through.

8 Garnish the dish with parsley sprigs, if desired, and serve immediately.

**NUTRITION**
Calories 559; Sugars 5 g; Protein 35 g;
Carbohydrate 24 g; Fat 37 g; Saturates 13 g

  easy

5 mins

1 hr

 **COOK'S TIP**

Serve this dish with plain boiled rice or noodles, if you wish.

Roasting the spices for this dish gives it a nice dark color and a richer flavor. Serve with chapatis and white lentils for a substantial meal.

# Sliced Beef *with* Yogurt

1 Place the beef in a large bowl. Combine with the yogurt, gingerroot, garlic, chili powder, turmeric, garam masala, salt, cardamoms, and black cumin seeds and set aside until required.

2 Dry-fry the ground almonds, desiccated coconut, poppy seeds, and sesame seeds in a heavy skillet until golden, shaking the pan occasionally.

3 Transfer the spice mixture to a food processor and process until finely ground. (Add 1 tablespoon water to blend, if necessary.) Add the ground spice mixture to the meat mixture and combine.

4 Heat a little oil in a large pan and cook the onions until golden brown. Remove the onions from the pan. Stir-fry the meat in the remaining oil for about 5 minutes, then return the onions to the pan, and stir-fry for a further 5–7 minutes. Add the water, cover, and simmer over low heat, stirring occasionally, for 25–30 minutes. Add the chiles and cilantro and serve hot.

**SERVES 4**

1 lb/450 g lean beef slices, cut into 1-inch/2.5-cm slices
5 tbsp natural yogurt
1 tsp finely chopped fresh gingerroot
1 tsp crushed garlic
1 tsp chili powder
pinch of ground turmeric
2 tsp garam masala
1 tsp salt
2 cardamoms
1 tsp black cumin seeds
2/3 cups ground almonds
1 tbsp dry unsweetened coconut
1 tbsp poppy seeds
1 tbsp sesame seeds
1 1/4 cups vegetable oil
2 medium onions, chopped finely
1 1/4 cups water
2 fresh red chiles, sliced thinly
few fresh cilantro leaves, chopped

**NUTRITION**
Calories *981*; Sugars *5 g*; Protein *33 g*;
Carbohydrate *6 g*; Fat *94 g*; Saturates *14 g*

 easy

 20 mins

20 mins

45 mins

If tomatillos are not available, use fresh tomatoes and bottled green salsa instead, and add a good hit of lime juice at the end.

# Chile Verde

**SERVES 4**

2 lb 4 oz/1 kg pork, cut into bite-size chunks
1 onion, chopped
2 bay leaves
1 garlic bulb, cut in half
1 bouillon cube
2 garlic cloves, chopped
1 lb/450 g oz fresh tomatillos, husks removed, cooked in a small amount of water until just tender, then chopped, or 1 lb/450 g canned tomatillos
2 large fresh mild green chiles, such as anaheim, or a combination of 1 green bell pepper and 2 jalapeño chiles, deseeded and chopped
3 tbsp vegetable oil
1 cup pork or chicken bouillon
½ tsp mild chili powder
½ tsp cumin
4–6 tbsp chopped fresh cilantro, to garnish

*to serve*
warmed flour tortillas
lime wedges

**NUTRITION**
Calories *433*; Sugars *6 g*; Protein *56 g*;
Carbohydrate *9 g*; Fat *19 g*; Saturates *4 g*

  moderate

10 mins

1 hr 30 mins

1 Place the pork in a large pan with the onion, bay leaves, and garlic bulb. Add water to cover and bring to a boil. Skim off the froth from the surface and add the bouillon cube, stirring well to mix and dissolve. Reduce the heat to very low and simmer for about 1½ hours or until the meat is very tender.

2 Meanwhile, put the chopped garlic in a blender or food processor with the tomatillos and green chiles, and bell pepper, if using. Process to a purée.

3 Heat the oil in a pan, add the tomatillo mixture, and cook over medium-high heat for about 10 minutes or until thickened. Add the bouillon, chili powder, and cumin.

4 When the meat is tender, discard the garlic bulb and bay leaves, remove from the pan, and add to the sauce. Simmer gently to combine the flavors.

5 Garnish with the chopped cilantro and serve with tortillas and lime wedges.

This khorma, a traditional northern Indian recipe, has a thick, richly flavored and creamy textured sauce and is quite simple to cook.

# Beef Khorma *with* Almonds

**1** Heat the oil in a pan. Add the onions and stir-fry until golden brown. Remove half of the onions from the pan, set aside, and reserve.

**2** Add the meat to the remaining onions in the pan and stir-fry for about 5 minutes. Remove the pan from the heat.

**3** Combine the garam masala, ground coriander, gingerroot, garlic, salt, and yogurt in a bowl. Gradually add the meat to the spice mixture and mix to coat well. Return the meat mixture to the pan. Cook, stirring constantly, for 5–7 minutes or until the mixture is golden.

**4** Add the cloves, cardamoms, and peppercorns. Add the water, lower the heat, cover the pan, and then simmer for approximately 45–60 minutes. If necessary, add another 1¼ cups water and cook for another 10–15 minutes, stirring occasionally.

**5** Just before serving, garnish with the reserved onions, chopped almonds, green chiles, and the fresh cilantro leaves. Serve with chapatis.

**SERVES 4**

1¼ cups vegetable oil
3 medium onions, chopped finely
2¼ lbs/1 kg lean beef, cubed
1½ tsp garam masala
1½ tsp ground coriander
1½ tsp chopped finely fresh gingerroot
1½ tsp crushed garlic
1 tsp salt
⅔ cup natural yogurt
2 cloves
3 green cardamoms
4 black peppercorns
2½ cups water
chapatis, to serve

*to garnish*
6 almonds, soaked, peeled, and chopped
2 fresh green chiles, chopped
few fresh cilantro leaves

**NUTRITION**
Calories 735; Sugars 6 g; Protein 41 g; Carbohydrate 9 g; Fat 60 g; Saturates 9 g

⭐⭐ easy
🕐 20 mins
🕐 1 hr 30 mins

Thai food has become so popular in recent years that most ingredients can be found in your local supermarket.

# Red Pork Curry

**SERVES 4–6**

2 lb/900 g boned pork shoulder, sliced
3 cups coconut milk
2 fresh red chiles, seeded and sliced
2 tbsp Thai fish sauce
2 tsp brown sugar
1 large red bell pepper, seeded and sliced
6 kaffir lime leaves, shredded
½ bunch fresh mint leaves, shredded
½ bunch Thai basil leaves, shredded

*red curry paste*

1 tbsp coriander seeds
2 tsp cumin seeds
2 tsp black or white peppercorns
1 tsp salt
5–8 dried hot red chiles
3–4 shallots, chopped
6–8 garlic cloves
2-inch/5-cm piece of fresh gingerroot, chopped
2 tsp kaffir lime rind or 2 kaffir lime leaves
1 tbsp ground red chili powder
1 tbsp shrimp paste
2 lemongrass stalks, sliced thinly

**NUTRITION**
Calories *398*; Sugars *12 g*; Protein *38 g*;
Carbohydrate *47 g*; Fat *9 g*; Saturates *3 g*

✪✪✪     moderate

🕐     15 mins

🕐     45 mins

1 To make the red curry paste, grind the coriander seeds, cumin seeds, peppercorns, and salt to a fine powder in a mortar with a pestle. Add the chiles, one at a time, according to taste, until ground.

2 Put the shallots, garlic, gingerroot, kaffir lime rind or leaves, chili powder, and shrimp paste in a food processor. Process for about 1 minute. Add the ground spices and process again. Adding water, a few drops at a time, continue to process until a thick paste forms. Scrape the mixture into a bowl and stir in the lemongrass.

3 Put about half the red curry paste in a large deep heavy skillet with the pork. Cook over medium heat, stirring gently, for 2–3 minutes until the pork is evenly coated and begins to brown.

4 Stir in the coconut milk and bring to a boil. Cook, stirring frequently, for about 10 minutes. Reduce the heat, stir in the chiles, Thai fish sauce, and brown sugar, and simmer for about 20 minutes. Add the red bell pepper and simmer for a further 10 minutes.

5 Chop the lime leaves and add to the curry with half the mint and basil. Transfer to a serving dish, sprinkle with the remaining mint and basil, and serve the curry with the rice.

This dish is a meal in itself, containing both meat and potatoes cooked in a herby wine gravy. A selection of fresh vegetables may be served with the dish, if wished.

# Potato *and* Sausage Panfry

1 Cook the cubed potatoes in a saucepan of boiling water for 10 minutes or until softened. Drain thoroughly and set aside.

2 Melt the butter in a large skillet. Add the sausages and cook for 5 minutes, turning them frequently to ensure that they brown on all sides.

3 Add the bacon slices, onion, zucchini and potatoes to the pan. Cook the mixture for a further 10 minutes, stirring the mixture and turning the sausages frequently.

4 Stir in the white wine, bouillon, Worcestershire sauce, and chopped mixed herbs. Season with salt and pepper to taste and cook the mixture over a gentle heat for 10 minutes. Add more salt and pepper, if necessary.

5 Transfer the potato and sausage pan-fry to warm serving plates, garnish with chopped fresh herbs, and serve at once.

**SERVES 4**

1½ lb/675 g potatoes, cubed
2 tbsp butter
8 large herb sausages
4 smoked bacon slices
1 onion, quartered
1 zucchini, sliced
⅔ cup dry white wine
1¼ cups vegetable bouillon
1 tsp Worcestershire sauce
2 tbsp chopped mixed fresh herbs
salt and pepper
chopped fresh herbs, to garnish

**NUTRITION**
Calories 774; Sugars 9 g; Protein 31 g;
Carbohydrate 50 g; Fat 48 g; Saturates 15 g

easy

15 mins

35 mins

**COOK'S TIP**

Use different flavors of sausage to vary the dish—there are many different varieties available.

Tender, lean pork, cooked in a tasty, rich tomato sauce, is flavored with the extra tang of plain yogurt.

# Pork Stroganoff

**SERVES 4**

12 oz/350 g lean pork tenderloin
1 tbsp vegetable oil
1 medium onion, chopped
2 garlic cloves, crushed
¼ cup all-purpose flour
2 tbsp tomato paste
2 cups Fresh Chicken or Fresh Vegetable Bouillon (see page 14)
1¾ cups sliced white mushrooms
1 large green bell pepper, seeded and diced
½ tsp ground nutmeg, plus extra to garnish
4 tbsp low-fat plain yogurt, plus extra to serve
salt and pepper
white rice, freshly boiled, to serve
ground nutmeg to garnish

1 Trim away any excess fat and membrane from the pork, then cut the meat into slices ½-inch/1-cm thick.

2 Heat the oil in a large pan. Add the pork, onion, and garlic and cook over low heat, stirring occasionally, for 4–5 minutes until lightly browned.

3 Stir in the flour and tomato paste, pour in the bouillon, and stir to mix.

4 Add the mushrooms, green bell pepper, and nutmeg and season to taste with salt and pepper. Bring to a boil, cover, and simmer for 20 minutes until the pork is tender and cooked through.

5 Remove the pan from the heat, cool slightly, then stir in the yogurt.

6 Serve the pork and sauce on a bed of rice, with an extra spoonful of yogurt, and garnish with a dusting of ground nutmeg.

**NUTRITION**
Calories 223; Sugars 7 g; Protein 22 g; Carbohydrate 12 g; Fat 10 g; Saturates 3 g

easy
2 hrs 15 mins
30 mins

 **COOK'S TIP**

You can buy ready-made bouillon from leading supermarkets. Although more expensive, they are more nutritious than bouillon cubes, which are high in salt and artificial flavorings.

This is a very simple dish which lends itself to almost any combination of vegetables that you have to hand.

# Pork Stir-Fry *with* Vegetables

1 Heat the oil in a preheated wok. Add the garlic, ginger, and pork. Stir-fry for 1–2 minutes until the meat is sealed.

2 Add the carrot, bell pepper, fennel, and water chestnuts and stir-fry for about 2–3 minutes.

3 Add the bean sprouts and stir-fry for 1 minute. Remove the pork and vegetables, set aside, and keep warm.

4 Add the Chinese rice wine, pork or chicken bouillon, and sugar to the wok. Blend the cornstarch to a smooth paste with the water and stir it into the sauce. Bring to a boil, stirring constantly until thickened and clear.

5 Return the meat and vegetables to the wok and cook for 1–2 minutes until heated through and coated with the sauce. Serve immediately.

**SERVES 4**

12 oz/350 g lean pork tenderloin, sliced thinly
2 tbsp vegetable oil
2 garlic cloves, crushed
1/2-inch/1-cm piece of fresh gingerroot, cut into slivers
1 carrot, cut into thin strips
1 red bell pepper, seeded and diced
1 fennel bulb, sliced
5 water chestnuts, halved
1 1/2 cups bean sprouts
2 tbsp Chinese rice wine
1 1/4 cups pork or chicken bouillon
pinch of dark brown sugar
1 tsp cornstarch
2 tsp water

**NUTRITION**
Calories *216*; Sugars *3 g*; Protein *19 g*; Carbohydrate *5 g*; Fat *12 g*; Saturates *3 g*

 moderate

5 mins

15 mins

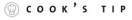 **COOK'S TIP**

Use dry sherry instead of Chinese rice wine if you have difficulty obtaining it.

Prunes add an earthy, wine flavor to this spicy stew. Serve with tortillas or crusty bread to dip into the rich sauce.

# Spicy Pork *with* Prunes

**SERVES 4**

3¼ lb/1.5 kg pork joint, such as leg or
  shoulder
juice of 2–3 limes
10 garlic cloves, chopped
3–4 tbsp mild chili powder
4 tbsp vegetable oil
2 onions, chopped
2¼ cups chicken bouillon
25 small tart tomatoes, chopped coarsely
25 prunes, pitted
1–2 tsp sugar
pinch of ground cinnamon
pinch of ground allspice
pinch of ground cumin
salt
warmed corn tortillas, to serve

1 Combine the pork with the lime juice, garlic, chili powder, 2 tablespoons of oil, and salt. Set aside to marinate in the refrigerator overnight.

2 Remove the pork from the marinade. Wipe the pork dry with paper towels and reserve the marinade. Heat the remaining oil in a flameproof casserole and brown the pork evenly until just golden. Add the onions, the reserved marinade, and bouillon. Cover and cook in a preheated oven, 350°F/180°C, for about 2–3 hours until tender.

3 Spoon off fat from the surface of the cooking liquid and add the tomatoes. Continue to cook for about 20 minutes until the tomatoes are tender. Mash the tomatoes into a coarse purée. Add the prunes and sugar, then adjust the seasoning, adding cinnamon, allspice, and cumin to taste, as well as extra chili powder, if wished.

4 Increase the oven temperature to 400°F/200°C and return the meat and sauce to the oven for another 20–30 minutes or until the meat has browned on top and the juices have thickened.

5 Remove the meat and set aside for a few minutes. Carefully carve it into thin slices and spoon the sauce over the top. Serve warm with corn tortillas.

**NUTRITION**
Calories *352*; Sugars *1 g*; Protein *39 g*;
Carbohydrate *24 g*; Fat *12 g*; Saturates *2 g*

moderate

8 hrs 15 mins

3–4 hrs

Dried cannellini beans feature in many Italian, Spanish, French, and Greek stews and casseroles, especially during the winter months.

# Basque Pork *and* Beans

1 Drain the cannellini beans and put in a large pan with fresh water to cover. Bring to a boil and boil rapidly for 10 minutes. Lower the heat and simmer for 20 minutes. Drain and set aside.

2 Add enough oil to cover the base of a skillet in a very thin layer. Heat the oil over medium heat, add a few pieces of the pork, and fry on all sides until brown. Remove and set aside. Repeat with the remaining pork.

3 Add 1 tablespoon oil to the skillet, if necessary, then add the onion and cook for 3 minutes. Stir in the garlic and cook for another 2 minutes. Return the pork to the skillet.

4 Add the tomatoes and bring to a boil. Lower the heat, stir in the bell pepper slices, orange rind, and the drained beans. Season with salt and pepper.

5 Transfer the contents of the pan to a casserole. Cover the casserole and cook in a preheated oven, 350°F/180°c, for 45 minutes until the beans and pork are both tender. Sprinkle with chopped fresh parsley and serve immediately, straight from the casserole.

**SERVES 4**

1 cup dried cannellini beans, soaked in cold water overnight
olive oil, for frying
1¼ lb/600 g boneless leg of pork, cut into 2-inch/5-cm chunks
1 large onion, sliced
3 large garlic cloves, crushed
14 oz/400 g canned chopped tomatoes
2 green bell peppers, seeded and sliced
finely grated rind of 1 large orange
salt and pepper
finely chopped fresh parsley, to garnish

**NUTRITION**
Calories 352; Sugars 1 g; Protein 39 g; Carbohydrate 24 g; Fat 12 g; Saturates 2 g

      easy

    8 hr 15 mins

    1 hr 30 mins

Served with rice and spicy vegetables, this dish is a great success at dinner parties.

# Lamb Pot Roast

**SERVES 4**

5½ lb/2.5 kg leg of lamb
2 tsp fresh gingerroot, chopped finely
2 tsp fresh garlic, crushed
2 tsp garam masala
1 tsp salt
2 tsp black cumin seeds
4 black peppercorns
3 cloves
1 tsp chili powder
3 tbsp lemon juice
1¼ cups oil
1 large onion, peeled
8–10 cups water

1 Remove the fat from the lamb. Prick the lamb all over with a fork.

2 In a bowl, mix the gingerroot, garlic, garam masala, salt, black cumin seeds, peppercorns, cloves, and chilli powder until well combined. Stir in the lemon juice and mix well. Rub the mixture all over the leg of lamb and set aside.

3 Heat the oil in a pan. Place the meat in the pan and place the onion alongside.

4 Add enough water to cover the meat and cook over low heat for 2½–3 hours, turning occasionally. (If, after a while, the water has evaporated and the meat is not tender, add a little extra water.) Once the water has completely evaporated, turn the roast over to brown it on all sides.

5 Remove the roast from the pan and transfer to a serving dish. Cut the roast into slices or serve it whole to be carved at the table. Serve hot or cold.

**NUTRITION**

Calories *661*; Sugars *44 g*; Protein *47 g*; Carbohydrate *1 g*; Fat *53 g*; Saturates *10 g*

 easy

 20 mins

 2½–3 hrs

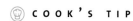 **COOK'S TIP**

Traditionally, a pan called a *degchi* is used for pot-roasting in India. It is set over hot ashes and contains hot coals in its lid.

The sweet, spicy blend of cinnamon, coriander, and cumin is the perfect complement to the tender lamb and apricots in this warming casserole.

# Fruity Lamb Casserole

1 Place the meat in a mixing bowl and add the cinnamon, coriander, cumin, and oil. Mix thoroughly so that the lamb is well coated in the spices.

2 Heat a non–stick skillet for a few seconds, then add the lamb. Reduce the heat and cook for 4–5 minutes, stirring, until browned all over. Transfer the lamb to a large casserole.

3 In the same skillet, cook the onion, garlic, tomatoes, and tomato paste for 5 minutes. Season to taste with salt and pepper. Stir in the apricots and sugar, add the bouillon, and bring to a boil.

4 Spoon the sauce over the lamb and mix well. Cover and cook in a preheated oven, 350°F/180°C, for 1 hour, removing the lid for the last 10 minutes.

5 Coarsely chop the cilantro and sprinkle it over the casserole to garnish. Serve the lamb straight from the casserole with brown rice, steamed couscous, or bulgar wheat.

**SERVES 4**

1 lb/450 g lean lamb, trimmed and cut into 1-inch/2.5-cm cubes
1 tsp ground cinnamon
1 tsp ground coriander
1 tsp ground cumin
2 tsp olive oil
1 red onion, chopped finely
1 garlic clove, crushed
14 oz/400 g canned chopped tomatoes
2 tbsp tomato paste
4½ oz/125 g no-soak dried apricots
1 tsp superfine sugar
1¼ cups vegetable bouillon
salt and pepper
1 small bunch fresh cilantro, to garnish
brown rice, steamed couscous, or bulgar wheat, to serve

**NUTRITION**
Calories *384*; Sugars *16 g*; Protein *32 g*; Carbohydrate *17 g*; Fat *22 g*; Saturates *9 g*

easy

5 mins

1 hr 15 mins

A big pot of "cocido" is warming on a cold day, great for a family meal. Serve with a selection of several salsas and a stack of corn tortillas.

# Simmered Medley

### SERVES  6 – 8

2 lb/900 g boneless pork
2 bay leaves
1 onion, chopped
8 garlic cloves, chopped finely
2 tbsp chopped fresh cilantro
1 carrot, sliced thinly
2 celery stalks, diced
2 chicken bouillon cubes
½ chicken, cut into portions
4–5 ripe tomatoes, diced
½ tsp mild chili powder
grated rind of ¼ orange
¼ tsp ground cumin
juice of 3 oranges
1 zucchini, cut into bite-size pieces
¼ cabbage, sliced thinly and blanched
1 apple, cut into bite-size pieces
about 10 prunes, pitted
¼ tsp ground cinnamon
pinch of ground ginger
2 hard chorizo sausages, about 12 oz/350 g in
    total, cut into bite-size pieces
salt and pepper

### NUTRITION
Calories 555; Sugars 17 g; Protein 47 g;
Carbohydrate 19 g; Fat 33 g; Saturates 12 g

  moderate

20 mins

2 hrs 15 mins

1 Combine the pork, bay leaves, onion, garlic, cilantro, carrot, and celery in a large pan and fill with cold water. Bring to a boil, then skim off the froth on the surface. Reduce the heat and simmer for 1 hour.

2 Add the bouillon cubes to the pan with the chicken, tomatoes, chili powder, orange rind, and cumin. Cook for another 45 minutes or until the chicken is tender. Spoon off the fat that forms on the top.

3 Add the orange juice, zucchini, cabbage, apple, prunes, cinnamon, gingerroot, and chorizo. Simmer for a further 20 minutes or until the zucchini is soft and tender and the chorizo is completely cooked through.

4 Season with salt and pepper to taste. Serve with rice, tortillas, and salsa.

This type of dish is popular in the Balkans, through Russia, to the Middle East. The saffron and pomegranate juice give it an exotic flavor.

# Azerbaijani Lamb Pilaf

1 Heat the oil in a large flameproof casserole or wide pan over high heat. Add the lamb, in batches, and cook stirring and turning frequently, for about 7 minutes until lightly browned.

2 Add the onions, reduce the heat to medium-high, and cook for about 2 minutes until beginning to soften. Add the cumin and rice and cook, stirring to coat, for about 2 minutes until the rice is translucent. Stir in the tomato paste and the saffron threads.

3 Add the pomegranate juice and bouillon and bring to a boil, stirring. Stir in the apricots or prunes and raisins. Reduce the heat to low, cover, and simmer for 20–25 minutes until the lamb and rice are tender and the liquid has been absorbed.

4 Season to taste, sprinkle the chopped mint and watercress over the pilaf, and serve from the casserole.

**SERVES 4 – 6**

2–3 tbsp vegetable oil

1½ lbs/675 g boneless lamb shoulder, cut into 1-inch/2.5-cm cubes

2 onions, coarsely chopped

1 tsp ground cumin

1 cup risotto, long-grain, or basmati rice

1 tbsp tomato paste

1 tsp saffron threads

scant ½ cup pomegranate juice (see Cook's Tip)

3½ cups lamb or chicken bouillon or water

½ cup dried apricots or prunes, ready soaked and halved

2 tbsp raisins

salt and pepper

*to serve*

2 tbsp chopped fresh mint

2 tbsp chopped fresh watercress

**NUTRITION**

Calories 399; Sugars 19 g; Protein 25 g; Carbohydrate 45 g; Fat 13 g; Saturates 4 g

 easy

 15 mins

50 mins

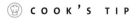 **COOK'S TIP**

Pomegranate juice is available from Middle Eastern grocery stores. If you cannot find it, substitute unsweetened grape or apple juice.

This curry uses the typically red-hot chili flavor of Thai red curry paste, made with dried red chiles, to give it a warm, russet-red color.

# Red Lamb Curry

**SERVES 4**

1 lb/450 g boneless lean leg of lamb
2 tbsp vegetable oil
1 large onion, sliced
2 garlic cloves, crushed
2 tbsp Thai red curry paste
²/₃ cup coconut milk
1 tbsp brown sugar
1 large red bell pepper, seeded and sliced thickly
½ cup lamb or beef bouillon
1 tbsp Thai fish sauce
2 tbsp lime juice
8 oz/225 g can water chestnuts, drained
2 tbsp chopped fresh cilantro
2 tbsp chopped fresh basil
salt and pepper
boiled jasmine rice, to serve
fresh basil leaves, to garnish

1 Trim the meat and cut it into 1¼-inch/3-cm cubes. Heat the oil in a large skillet or wok over high heat and stir-fry the onion and garlic for 2–3 minutes to soften. Add the meat and stir-fry until lightly browned.

2 Stir in the curry paste and cook for a few seconds, then add the coconut milk and sugar and bring to a boil. Reduce the heat and simmer for 15 minutes, stirring occasionally.

3 Stir in the red bell pepper, bouillon, fish sauce, and lime juice, cover, and continue simmering for another 15 minutes or until the meat is tender.

4 Add the water chestnuts, cilantro, and basil, adjust the seasoning to taste. Garnish with fresh basil leaves and serve with jasmine rice.

**NUTRITION**
Calories 363; Sugars 11 g; Protein 29 g;
Carbohydrate 21 g; Fat 19 g; Saturates 6 g

moderate

 10 mins

 40 mins

Cooked on festive occasions, especially for weddings, lamb biryani is among the most popular dishes in India. The meat can be cooked in advance and added to the rice on the day of the party.

# Lamb Biryani

1 Boil the milk in a pan with the saffron and set aside. Heat the ghee in a pan and fry the onions until golden. Remove half of the onions and ghee from the pan and set aside in a bowl.

2 Combine the meat, yogurt, gingerroot, garlic, garam masala, 1 tsp salt, and turmeric in a large bowl and mix well.

3 Return the pan with the ghee and onions to the heat, add the meat mixture, stir for about 3 minutes, and add the water. Cook over low heat for 45 minutes, stirring occasionally. Check to see whether the meat is tender: if not, add ⅔ cup water and cook for 15 minutes. Once all the water has evaporated, stir-fry for about 2 minutes and set aside.

4 Meanwhile, place the rice in a pan. Add the cumin seeds, cardamoms, salt, and enough water for cooking, and cook over medium heat until the rice is half-cooked. Drain. Remove half of the rice and place in a bowl.

5 Spoon the meat mixture on top of the rice in the pan. Add half each of the saffron mixture, lemon juice, chiles, and cilantro. Add the other half of the rice, saffron, lemon juice, chiles, and cilantro. Cover and cook over low heat for 15–20 minutes or until the rice is cooked. Stir well and serve hot.

SERVES 4 – 6

⅔ cup milk
1 tsp saffron
5 tbsp ghee
3 medium onions, sliced
2¼ lbs/1 kg lean lamb, cubed
7 tbsp natural yogurt
1½ tsp fresh gingerroot, chopped finely
1½ tsp crushed fresh garlic
2 tsp garam masala
2 tsp salt
¼ tsp turmeric
2½ cups water
2½ cups basmati rice
2 tsp black cumin seeds
3 cardamoms
4 tbsp lemon juice
2 fresh green chiles
¼ bunch fresh cilantro

NUTRITION
Calories 1073; Sugars 14 g; Protein 66 g; Carbohydrate 108 g; Fat 42 g; Saturates 23 g

 easy

 15 mins

 1 hr 45 mins

Venison is super-lean and low in fat, so it's the perfect choice for a healthy diet. Cooked quickly with crisp vegetables, it's ideal in a stir-fry.

# Sweet *and* Sour Venison Stir-Fry

**SERVES 4**

1 bunch scallions
1 red bell pepper
1⅓ cups snow peas
10 baby corn cobs
12 oz/350 g lean venison steak
1 tbsp vegetable oil
1 garlic clove, crushed
1-inch/2.5-cm piece fresh gingerroot, chopped finely
3 tbsp light soy sauce, plus extra for serving
1 tbsp white wine vinegar
2 tbsp dry sherry
2 tsp honey
8 oz/225 g canned pineapple pieces in natural juice, drained
½ cup bean sprouts
freshly cooked rice, to serve

1 Cut the scallions into 1-inch/2.5-cm pieces. Halve and seed the red bell pepper and cut it into 1-inch/2.5-cm pieces. Trim the snow peas and baby corn cobs. Set aside.

2 Trim the meat and cut it into thin strips. Heat the oil in a large skillet or wok until hot and stir-fry the meat, garlic, and gingerroot for 5 minutes.

3 Add the scallions, red bell pepper, snow peas, and baby corn cobs, then stir in the soy sauce, vinegar, sherry, and honey. Stir-fry for another 5 minutes.

4 Carefully stir in the pineapple pieces and bean sprouts and cook for another 1–2 minutes to heat through. Serve with freshly cooked rice and extra soy sauce for dipping.

**NUTRITION**
Calories *219*; Sugars *18 g*; Protein *23 g*; Carbohydrate *20 g*; Fat *5 g*; Saturates *1 g*

⭐     very easy

🕐     15 mins

🕐     15 mins

👨‍🍳 **COOK'S TIP**

For a nutritious meal-in-one, cook 8 oz/225 g egg noodles in boiling water for 3–4 minutes. Drain and add to the pan at Step 4, with the pineapple and bean sprouts an extra 2 tablespoons soy sauce.

Polenta can be served fresh, as in this dish, or it can be cooled, then sliced, and broiled or fried.

# Polenta *with* Rabbit Stew

1 Grease a large casserole with a little butter. Mix the polenta, salt, and water in a large pan, whisking well to prevent lumps from forming. Bring to a boil over medium heat and boil for 10 minutes, stirring vigorously and constantly. Turn into the prepared casserole and bake in a preheated oven, 375°F/190°C, for 40 minutes.

2 Meanwhile, heat the oil in a large pan and add the rabbit pieces, garlic, and shallots. Fry for 10 minutes until browned.

3 Stir in the wine and cook for a further 5 minutes.

4 Add the carrot, celery, bay leaves, rosemary, tomatoes, olives, and 1¼ cups water. Cover the pan and simmer for about 45 minutes or until the rabbit is tender. Season with salt and pepper to taste.

5 To serve, spoon or cut a portion of polenta and place on each serving plate. Top with a ladleful of rabbit stew. Serve immediately.

**SERVES 4**

butter, for greasing
1¾ cups polenta or cornmeal
1 tbsp coarse sea salt
5 cups water
4 tbsp olive oil
4 lb 8 oz/2 kg rabbit joints
3 garlic cloves, peeled
3 shallots, sliced
⅔ cup red wine
1 carrot, sliced
1 celery stalk, sliced
2 bay leaves
1 fresh rosemary sprig
3 tomatoes, peeled and diced
¾ cup pitted black olives
salt and pepper

**NUTRITION**
Calories *726*; Sugars *2 g*; Protein *61 g*;
Carbohydrate *55 g*; Fat *25 g*; Saturates *6 g*

 moderate

 20 mins

1 hr 45 mins

# Poultry

Chicken is the perfect choice for one-pot cooking, because there are so many different cuts to choose from, from inexpensive thighs to delicate breast meat, as well as the whole bird. In addition, as it is often rather bland in flavor, it benefits from being combined with vegetables, fruit, herbs, and aromatics. Almost everyone loves chicken and the recipes in this chapter reflect its universal popularity with dishes from Mexico, India, Thailand, Spain, Italy, and the Middle East, among other countries. It is a versatile meat and can be cooked in any number of ways, from casseroles to stir-fries and from risottos to curries. There are recipes for all occasions and every time of year, from Sunday lunch with the family to an al fresco dinner party. Hot and spicy, rich and creamy, filling and flavorful, subtle and delicate—there is a one-pot chicken dish that is sure to please.

This hearty and nourishing soup, combining garbanzo beans and chicken, is an ideal starter for a family supper.

# Chicken *and* Garbanzo Bean Soup

**SERVES   4**

2 tbsp butter
3 scallions, chopped
2 garlic cloves, chopped finely
1 fresh marjoram sprig, chopped finely
5 cups chicken bouillon
12 oz boned chicken breasts, diced
1½ cup canned garbanzo beans, drained
1 bouquet garni
salt and white pepper
1 red bell pepper, diced
1 green bell pepper, diced
1 cup small dried pasta shapes, such as elbow macaroni
croutons, to serve

1 Melt the butter in a large pan. Add the scallions, garlic, marjoram, and chicken, and cook, stirring frequently, over medium heat for 5 minutes.

2 Add the chicken bouillon, garbanzo beans, and bouquet garni to the pan and season to taste with salt and white pepper.

3 Bring the soup to a boil, lower the heat, and simmer gently for about 1 hour.

4 Add the diced bell peppers and pasta to the pan, then simmer the soup for another 20 minutes.

5 Transfer the soup to a warm tureen. To serve, ladle the soup into individual serving bowls and serve immediately, garnished with croutons.

**NUTRITION**
Calories *347*; Sugars *2 g*; Protein *28 g*;
Carbohydrate *37 g*; Fat *11 g*; Saturates *4 g*

 moderate

 15 mins

1 hr 45 mins

 **COOK'S TIP**

If you prefer, you can use dried garbanzo beans. Cover with cold water and set aside to soak for 5–8 hours. Drain and add the beans to the soup, according to the recipe, and allow an additional 30 minutes–1 hour cooking time.

This soup evolved from the foodstalls that line the streets of Tlalpan, a suburb of Mexico City: avocado, chicken, and chiles provide a typically Mexican flavor.

# Chicken *and* Chipotle Soup

1 Place the bouillon, garlic, and chipotle chiles in a pan and bring to a boil.

2 Meanwhile, cut the avocado in half around the pit. Twist apart, then remove the pit with a knife. Carefully peel off the skin, dice the flesh, and toss in lime or lemon juice to prevent the flesh from turning brown.

3 Arrange the scallions, chicken, avocado, and fresh cilantro in the base of 4 individual soup bowls or in a large tureen.

4 Ladle the hot bouillon into the bowls and serve with lime wedges and a handful of tortilla chips if using.

**SERVES 4**

6¾ cups chicken bouillon

2–3 garlic cloves, chopped finely

1–2 chipotle chiles, cut into very thin strips (see Cook's Tip)

1 avocado

lime or lemon juice, for tossing

3–5 scallions, sliced thinly

12–14 oz/350–400 g skinless, boneless cooked chicken breast portions, torn or cut into shreds or thin strips

2 tbsp chopped fresh cilantro

*to serve*

1 lime, cut into wedges

handful of tortilla chips (optional)

**NUTRITION**

Calories *216*; Sugars *1 g*; Protein *28 g*;
Carbohydrate *2 g*; Fat *11 g*; Saturates *2 g*

 very easy

 10 mins

5 mins

🍳 **COOK'S TIP**

Chipotle chiles are smoked and are available canned or dried. They add a distinctive smoky flavor to dishes and are very hot. Drain canned chipotles before using. Dried chipotles need to be reconstituted.

The vermicelli gives this Chinese-style soup an Italian twist. Use egg noodles if you prefer.

# Chicken, Noodle, *and* Corn Soup

**SERVES 4**

1 lb/450 g skinless, boneless chicken breasts, cut into strips
5 cups chicken bouillon
⅔ cup cream
salt and pepper
¾ cup dried vermicelli
1 tbsp cornstarch
3 tbsp milk
1 cup corn kernels

1 Put the chicken, bouillon, and cream into a large saucepan and bring to a boil over low heat. Reduce the heat slightly and simmer for about 20 minutes. Season the soup with salt and black pepper to taste.

2 Meanwhile, cook the vermicelli in lightly salted boiling water for 10–12 minutes, until just tender. Drain the pasta and keep warm.

3 In a small bowl, mix together the cornstarch and milk to make a smooth paste. Stir the cornstarch into the soup until thickened.

4 Add the corn and vermicelli to the pan and heat through.

5 Transfer the soup to a warm tureen or individual soup bowls and serve.

**NUTRITION**
Calories *401*; Sugars *6 g*; Protein *31 g*;
Carbohydrate *17 g*; Fat *24 g*; Saturates *13 g*

easy
5 mins
30 mins

**COOK'S TIP**

For crab and corn soup, substitute 1 lb/450 g cooked crab meat for the chicken breasts. Flake the crab meat well before adding it to the saucepan and reduce the cooking time by 10 minutes.

This delicately flavored summer soup is surprisingly easy to make, and tastes delicious.

# Lemon *and* Chicken Soup

1 Melt the butter in a large pan. Add the shallots, carrots, celery, and chicken and cook over low heat, stirring occasionally, for 8 minutes.

2 Thinly pare the lemons and blanch the rind in boiling water for 3 minutes. Squeeze the juice from the lemons.

3 Add the lemon rind and juice and the chicken bouillon to the pan. Bring slowly to a boil over low heat. Simmer for 40 minutes, stirring occasionally.

4 Add the spaghetti to the pan and cook for 15 minutes. Season to taste with salt and white pepper and add the cream. Heat through, but do not let the soup boil or it will curdle.

5 Pour the soup into a large serving bowl or individual soup bowls, garnish with the parsley and half slices of lemon, and serve immediately.

**SERVES 4**

4 tbsp butter
8 shallots, sliced thinly
2 carrots, sliced thinly
2 celery stalks, sliced thinly
8 oz/225 g skinless, boneless chicken breasts, chopped finely
3 lemons
5 cups chicken bouillon
8 oz/225 g dried spaghetti, broken into small pieces
2/3 cup heavy cream
salt and white pepper

*to garnish*
1 sprig of fresh parsley
3 lemon slices, halved

**NUTRITION**
Calories *506*; Sugars *4 g*; Protein *19 g*;
Carbohydrate *41 g*; Fat *31 g*; Saturates *19 g*

 easy

10 mins

1 hr 10 mins

 **COOK'S TIP**

You can prepare this soup in advance up to the end of Step 3, so that all you need do before serving is heat it through very gently before adding the pasta and the finishing touches.

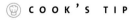

Any kind of rice is suitable for this soup—white or brown long-grain rice, or even wild rice. Leftover cooked rice is a handy addition for soups.

# Chicken *and* Rice Soup

**SERVES 4**

6½ cups chicken bouillon (see Cook's Tip)
2 small carrots, sliced very thinly
1 celery stalk, diced finely
1 baby leek, halved lengthwise and sliced thinly
1 cup small, young peas, thawed if frozen
1 cup cooked rice
5½ oz/150 g cooked chicken meat, sliced
2 tsp chopped fresh tarragon
1 tbsp chopped fresh parsley
salt and pepper
sprigs of fresh parsley, to garnish
crusty bread, to serve

1 Put the chicken bouillon in a large pan and add the carrots, celery, and leek. Bring to a boil, reduce the heat to low, partially cover, and simmer gently for 10 minutes until the vegetables are tender.

2 Stir in the peas, rice, and chicken meat and continue cooking for another 10–15 minutes or until the vegetables are tender.

3 Add the chopped tarragon and parsley and season to taste with salt and pepper as needed.

4 Ladle the soup into warmed bowls, garnish with fresh parsley sprigs, and serve immediately with crusty bread.

**NUTRITION**
Calories *165*; Sugars *3 g*; Protein *14 g*;
Carbohydrate *19 g*; Fat *4 g*; Saturates *1 g*

 very easy

 25 mins

 30 mins

🍴 **COOK'S TIP**

If the bouillon you are using is weak or if you have used a bouillon cube, add the herbs at the beginning, so they can flavor the bouillon for a longer time.

This soup makes a change from traditional chicken soup. It is spicy, and garnished with a generous quantity of cilantro leaves.

# Thai-Style Chicken *and* Coconut Soup

1 Put the bouillon in a pan with the chicken, chile, lemongrass, lime leaves, and gingerroot. Bring almost to a boil, reduce the heat, cover and simmer for 20–25 minutes, or until the chicken is cooked through.

2 Remove the chicken from the pan and strain the bouillon. When the chicken is cool, slice thinly, or shred into bite-size pieces.

3 Return the bouillon to the saucepan and heat to simmering. Stir in the coconut milk and scallions. Add the chicken and continue simmering for about 10 minutes, or until the soup is heated through and all the different flavors have mingled.

4 Stir in the chili paste. Season to taste with salt and, if wished, add a little more chili paste.

5 Ladle into warm bowls and float cilantro leaves on top to serve.

**SERVES 4**

5 cups chicken bouillon
7 oz/200 g skinless, boneless chicken
1 fresh chile, split lengthwise and seeded
3-inch/7.5-cm piece of lemongrass, split lengthwise
3–4 lime leaves
1-inch/2.5-cm piece of fresh gingerroot, peeled and sliced
½ cup coconut milk
6–8 scallions, sliced diagonally
¼ tsp chili paste, to taste
salt
fresh cilantro leaves, to garnish

**NUTRITION**
Calories *76*; Sugars *2 g*; Protein *13 g*; Carbohydrate *3 g*; Fat *1 g*; Saturates *0 g*

 easy

 5 mins

40 mins

🍳 **COOK'S TIP**

Once the bouillon is flavored and the chicken cooked, this soup is very quick to finish. If you wish, poach the chicken and strain the bouillon ahead of time. Store in the refrigerator separately.

This simple, Japanese style of cooking is ideal for thinly sliced breast of chicken. You can use thin turkey scallops, if you prefer.

# Teppanyaki

**SERVES 4**

4 boneless chicken breasts
1 red bell pepper
1 green bell pepper
4 scallions
8 baby corn cobs
generous cup bean sprouts
1 tbsp sesame or sunflower oil
4 tbsp shoyu or soy sauce
4 tbsp mirin
1 tbsp grated fresh gingerroot

1 Remove the skin from the chicken and slice at a slight angle, to a thickness of about $1/4$ inch/5 mm.

2 Seed and thinly slice the red and green bell peppers and trim and slice the scallions and corn cobs.

3 Arrange the bell peppers, scallions, corn cobs, and bean sprouts on a plate with the sliced chicken.

4 Heat a large griddle or heavy skillet, then lightly brush with sesame or sunflower oil. Add the vegetables and chicken slices, in small batches, allowing space between them so that they cook thoroughly.

5 Combine the shoyu or soy sauce, mirin, and gingerroot in a small serving bowl and serve as a dip with the chicken and vegetables.

**NUTRITION**
Calories *206*; Sugars *4 g*; Protein *30 g*;
Carbohydrate *6 g*; Fat *7 g*; Saturates *2 g*

easy

10 mins

10 mins

 **COOK'S TIP**

Mirin is a rich, sweet rice wine from Japan. You can buy it in Asian supermarkets, but if it is not available, add 1 tablespoon soft light brown sugar to the sauce instead.

Plain potato patties are a great favorite. Here, the potatoes are combined with ground chicken and mashed banana.

# Chicken *and* Banana Patties

1 Cook the diced potatoes in a pan of boiling water for about 10 minutes until tender. Drain well and mash until smooth. Stir in the ground chicken.

2 Mash the banana and add it to the potato with the flour, lemon juice, onion, and half of the chopped sage. Season to taste with salt and pepper and stir the mixture together.

3 Divide the mixture into 8 equal portions. With lightly floured hands, shape each portion into a round patty.

4 Heat the butter and oil in a skillet, add the chicken and banana patties and cook for 12–15 minutes or until cooked through, turning once. Remove from the skillet and keep warm.

5 Stir the cream and bouillon into the skillet with the remaining chopped sage. Cook over low heat for 2–3 minutes.

6 Arrange the patties on a warmed serving plate, garnish with fresh sage leaves, and serve immediately with the cream and sage sauce.

**SERVES 4**

1 lb/450 g potatoes, diced
8 oz/225 g ground chicken
1 large banana
2 tbsp all-purpose flour
1 tsp lemon juice
1 onion, chopped finely
2 tbsp chopped fresh sage
2 tbsp butter
2 tbsp vegetable oil
⅔ cup light cream
⅔ cup chicken bouillon
salt and pepper
fresh sage leaves, to garnish

**NUTRITION**
Calories *439*; Sugars *11 g*; Protein *22 g*; Carbohydrate *39 g*; Fat *23 g*; Saturates *10 g*

 moderate

5–10 mins

25–30 mins

🍳 **COOK'S TIP**

Do not boil the sauce once the cream has been added, or it will curdle. Cook it gently over very low heat.

This is a quick and tasty way to use leftover roast chicken. The sauce can also be used for any cooked poultry, lamb, or beef.

# Fragrant Chicken *and* Fava Beans

**SERVES 4**

1 tsp mustard oil
3 tbsp vegetable oil
1 large onion, chopped finely
3 garlic cloves, crushed
1 tbsp tomato paste
2 tomatoes, skinned and chopped
1 tsp ground turmeric
½ tsp cumin seeds, ground
½ tsp coriander seeds, ground
½ tsp chili powder
½ tsp garam masala
1 tsp red wine vinegar
1 small red bell pepper, chopped
4 oz/125 g frozen fava beans
1 lb/450 g cooked chicken, cut into bite-size pieces
salt
sprigs of fresh cilantro, to garnish

1 Heat the mustard oil in a large, skillet set over a high heat for approximately 1 minute, or until the oil begins to smoke.

2 Add the vegetable oil, reduce the heat, and then add the onion and the garlic. Fry the garlic and onion until they are golden.

3 Add the tomato paste, chopped tomatoes, turmeric, ground cumin, coriander seeds, chili powder, garam masala, and wine vinegar to the skillet. Stir the mixture until fragrant.

4 Add the red pepper and fava beans and stir for 2 minutes, or until the pepper is softened. Stir in the chicken, and salt to taste.

5 Simmer gently for 6–8 minute, or until the chicken is heated through and the beans are tender.

6 Serve as soon after cooking as possible, garnished with cilantro sprigs.

**NUTRITION**
Calories *270*; Sugars *3 g*; Protein *36 g*;
Carbohydrate *7 g*; Fat *11 g*; Saturates *2 g*

easy

25 mins

15 mins

**COOK'S TIP**

This dish is an ideal way of making use of any type of leftover poultry. Any variety of beans works well, but vegetables are just as useful, especially zucchini, potatoes, or broccoli.

Spices, herbs, fruit, nuts, and vegetables are combined to make an appealing casserole with lots of flavor.

# Spiced Chicken Casserole

1 Heat the olive oil in a large, heavy-based pan and add the chicken, shallots or pickling onions, and carrots. Cook, stirring frequently, over medium heat for about 6 minutes or until the chicken is browned.

2 Add the nuts, nutmeg, cinnamon, wine, bouillon, wine vinegar, herbs, orange rind, and sugar and season to taste with salt and pepper. Simmer over low heat for 2 hours until the meat is very tender. Stir the casserole occasionally.

3 Add the grapes just before serving and serve with wild rice or puréed potato. Garnish with herbs.

SERVES 4 – 6

3 tbsp olive oil
2 lb/900 g skinless, boneless chicken, sliced
10 shallots
3 carrots, chopped
6 chestnuts, sliced
½ cup slivered almonds, toasted
1 tsp freshly grated nutmeg
3 tsp ground cinnamon
1¼ cups white wine
1¼ cups chicken bouillon
¾ cup white wine vinegar
1 tbsp chopped fresh tarragon
1 tbsp chopped fresh flatleaf parsley
1 tbsp chopped fresh thyme
grated rind of 1 orange
1 tbsp dark muscovado sugar
1 cup seedless black grapes, halved
sea salt and pepper
fresh herbs, to garnish
wild rice or puréed potato, to serve

**NUTRITION**
Calories 385; Sugars 14 g; Protein 37 g; Carbohydrate 19 g; Fat 15 g; Saturates 2 g

 easy

10 mins

 2 hrs 15 mins

 **COOK'S TIP**

This casserole would also be delicious served with thick slices of crusty whole-wheat bread to soak up the sauce.

All the sunshine colors and flavors of Italy are combined in this easy and economical dish.

# Chicken Peperonata

**SERVES 4**

8 chicken thighs
2 tbsp whole-wheat flour
2 tbsp olive oil
1 small onion, sliced thinly
1 garlic clove, crushed
1 large red bell pepper, seeded and sliced thinly
1 large yellow bell pepper, seeded and sliced thinly
1 large green bell pepper. seeded and sliced thinly
14 oz/400 g canned chopped tomatoes
1 tbsp chopped fresh oregano
salt and pepper
fresh oregano, to garnish
crusty whole-wheat bread, to serve

1 Remove the skin from the chicken thighs and toss the meat in the flour.

2 Heat the oil in a wide skillet and fry the chicken over medium heat until sealed and lightly browned, then remove from the skillet.

3 Add the onion to the skillet, lower the heat, and cook, stirring occasionally, for about 5 minutes until softened, but not browned. Add the garlic, bell pepper slices, tomatoes, and oregano, then bring to a boil, stirring.

4 Arrange the chicken on top of the vegetables, season to taste with salt and pepper then cover the pan tightly, and simmer for 20–25 minutes or until the chicken is completely cooked and tender.

5 Taste and adjust the seasoning, if necessary. Transfer the chicken to a plate. Spoon the vegetables onto a warmed serving platter and top with the chicken. Garnish with fresh oregano and serve immediately with fresh, crusty whole-wheat bread.

**NUTRITION**
Calories 328; Sugars 7 g; Protein 35 g;
Carbohydrate 13 g; Fat 15 g; Saturates 4 g

easy

15 mins

40 mins

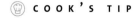 **COOK'S TIP**

For extra flavor, halve the peppers and broil under a preheated broiler until the skins are charred. Let cool then remove the skins and seeds. Slice the peppers thinly and use in the recipe.

A karahi is an extremely versatile two-handled metal pan, similar to a wok. Food is always cooked over high heat in a karahi.

# Karahi Chicken

1 Heat the ghee in a karahi, wok, or a large, heavy skillet. Add the garlic and onion. Stir-fry for about 4 minutes until the onion is golden.

2 Stir in the garam masala, ground coriander, mint, and bay leaf.

3 Add the chicken and cook over high heat, stirring occasionally, for about 5 minutes. Add the bouillon, lower the heat, and simmer for 10 minutes until the sauce has thickened and the chicken juices run clear when the meat is tested with the point of a sharp knife.

4 Stir in the chopped fresh cilantro and season with salt to taste, mix well, and serve immediately with warm nan bread or chapatis.

**SERVES 4**

2 tbsp ghee
3 garlic cloves, crushed
1 onion, chopped finely
2 tbsp garam masala
1 tsp coriander seeds, ground
½ tsp dried mint
1 bay leaf
1¾ lbs/785 g skinless, boneless chicken, diced
scant 1 cup chicken bouillon
1 tbsp chopped fresh cilantro
salt
warm nan bread or chapatis, to serve

**NUTRITION**
Calories 270; Sugars 1 g; Protein 41 g; Carbohydrate 1 g; Fat 11 g; Saturates 2 g

    easy

5 mins

20 mins

 **COOK'S TIP**

It is important to always heat a karahi or wok before you add the oil to help maintain the high temperature.

Fresh spring vegetables are the basis of this colorful casserole, which is topped with hearty whole-wheat biscuits.

# Springtime Chicken Pot Pie

**SERVES 4**

1 tbsp vegetable oil
8 skinless chicken drumsticks
1 small onion, sliced
2½ cups baby carrots
2 baby turnips
4 oz/125 g fava beans or peas
1 tsp cornstarch
1¼ cups chicken bouillon
2 bay leaves
salt and pepper

*biscuit topping*
2¼ cups whole-wheat flour
2 tsp baking powder
2 tbsp soft sunflower margarine
2 tsp dry whole-grain mustard
½ cup grated low-fat sharp Cheddar cheese
skim milk, to mix, plus extra for brushing
sesame seeds, for sprinkling

**NUTRITION**
Calories *560*; Sugars *10 g*; Protein *389 g*;
Carbohydrate *64 g*; Fat *18 g*; Saturates *4 g*

moderate

15 mins

1 hr 30 mins

1 Heat the oil in a large, heavy pan and fry the chicken, turning occasionally, until golden brown. Drain well and place in a casserole. Add the onion to the pan and cook, stirring occasionally, for 2–3 minutes until softened.

2 Cut the carrots and turnips into equal-size pieces. Add to the casserole with the onions and beans or peas.

3 Blend the cornstarch with a little of the bouillon, then stir in the rest, and heat gently, stirring until boiling. Pour into the casserole and add the bay leaves. Season to taste with salt and pepper.

4 Cover tightly and bake in a preheated oven, 400°F/200°C, for 50–60 minutes or until the chicken juices run clear when pierced with a skewer.

5 For the topping, sift the flour and baking powder. Mix in the margarine with a fork. Stir in the mustard, cheese, and enough milk to mix to a soft dough.

6 Roll out and cut 16 rounds with a 1½-inch/4-cm cookie cutter. Uncover the casserole, arrange the biscuit rounds on top of the chicken, then brush with milk, and sprinkle with sesame seeds. Return to the oven and bake for 20 minutes or until the topping is golden and firm.

Sweet bell peppers are typical of dishes from the Basque region in France. In this recipe, Bayonne ham, from the Pyrenees, adds a delicious flavor.

# Chicken Basquaise

1 Pat the chicken pieces dry with paper towels. Put 2 tablespoons flour in a plastic bag, season with salt and pepper, and add the chicken pieces. Seal the bag and shake to coat the chicken.

2 Heat 2 tablespoons of the oil in a large flameproof casserole over medium-high heat. Add the chicken and cook, turning frequently, for about 15 minutes until well browned all over. Transfer to a plate.

3 Heat the remaining oil in the casserole and add the onion and bell peppers. Reduce the heat to medium and stir-fry until beginning to color and soften. Add the garlic, chorizo, and tomato paste and cook, stirring constantly, for about 3 minutes. Add the rice and cook, stirring to coat, for about 2 minutes until the rice is translucent.

4 Add the bouillon, crushed chiles, and thyme, season to taste with salt and pepper, and stir well. Bring to a boil. Return the chicken to the casserole, pressing it gently into the rice. Cover and cook over very low heat for about 45 minutes until the chicken is cooked through and the rice is tender.

5 Gently stir the ham, black olives, and half the parsley into the rice mixture. Re-cover and heat through for a further 5 minutes. Sprinkle with the remaining parsley and serve immediately.

## SERVES 4 – 5

1 chicken, weighing 3 lb/1.35 kg, cut into 8 pieces
all-purpose flour, for dusting
2–3 tbsp olive oil
1 Bermuda onion, sliced thickly
2 red or yellow bell peppers, seeded and cut lengthwise into thick strips
2 garlic cloves
5½ oz/150 g spicy chorizo sausage, peeled and cut into ½-inch/1-cm pieces
1 tbsp tomato paste
1 cup long-grain white rice
2 cups chicken bouillon
1 tsp chile flakes
½ tsp dried thyme
¾ cup diced Bayonne or other air-dried ham
12 dry-cured black olives
2 tbsp chopped fresh flatleaf parsley
salt and pepper

## NUTRITION
Calories 559; Sugars 8 g; Protein 50 g; Carbohydrate 44 g; Fat 21 g; Saturates 6 g

✪✪✪ moderate

15 mins

 1 hr 30 mins

This variation of the traditional beef dish has layers of pasta and chicken or turkey baked in red wine, tomatoes, and a delicious cheese sauce.

# Chicken Lasagna

### SERVES 4

9 sheets fresh or dried lasagna
butter, for greasing
1 tbsp olive oil
1 red onion, chopped finely
1 garlic clove, crushed
1⅓ cups mushrooms
12 oz/350 g chicken or turkey breast, cut into chunks
⅔ cup red wine, diluted with generous ⅓ cup water
generous 1 cup crushed tomatoes
1 tsp sugar

*béchamel sauce*

5 tbsp butter
generous ⅓ cup all-purpose flour
2½ cups milk
1 egg, beaten
¾ cup freshly grated Parmesan cheese
salt and pepper

### NUTRITION

Calories 550; Sugars 11 g; Protein 35 g;
Carbohydrate 34 g; Fat 29 g; Saturates 12 g

★★★      moderate

20 mins

1 hr 15 mins

1 Cook the lasagna sheets in a pan of boiling water according to the instructions on the package. Lightly grease a deep ovenproof dish.

2 Heat the oil in a pan. Add the onion and garlic and cook over low heat, stirring occasionally, for 3–4 minutes. Add the mushrooms and chicken and cook for 4 minutes or until the meat browns.

3 Add the wine, bring to a boil, then simmer for 5 minutes. Stir in the crushed tomatoes and sugar and cook for 3–5 minutes until the meat is tender and cooked through. The sauce should have thickened, but still be quite runny.

4 To make the béchamel sauce, melt the butter in a pan, stir in the flour and cook for 2 minutes, stirring constantly. Remove the pan from the heat and gradually add the milk, mixing to form a smooth sauce. Return the pan to the heat and bring to a boil, stirring until thickened. Let cool slightly, then beat in the egg and half of the cheese. Season to taste with salt and pepper.

5 Place 3 sheets of lasagna in the base of the dish and spread with half of the chicken mixture. Repeat the layers. Top with the last 3 sheets of lasagna, pour over the béchamel sauce, and sprinkle with the Parmesan. Bake in a preheated oven, 375°F/190°C, for 30 minutes until golden and the pasta is cooked. Serve immediately.

This recipe is a type of cottage pie and is just as versatile. Add vegetables and herbs of your choice, depending on what you have at hand.

# Quick Chicken Bake

1 Dry-fry the ground chicken, onion, and carrots in a nonstick saucepan for 5 minutes, stirring frequently.

2 Sprinkle the chicken with the flour and simmer for a further 2 minutes.

3 Gradually blend in the tomato paste and bouillon, then simmer gently for 15 minutes. Season to taste with salt and pepper and add the thyme.

4 Transfer the chicken and vegetable mixture to a casserole and let cool.

5 Spoon the mashed potato over the chicken mixture and sprinkle with the grated cheese.

6 Bake in a preheated oven, 400°F/200°C, for 20 minutes or until the cheese topping is bubbling and golden, then serve with the peas.

**SERVES 4**

1 lb/450 g ground chicken
1 large onion, chopped finely
2 carrots, diced finely
¼ cup all-purpose flour
1 tbsp tomato paste
1¼ cups chicken bouillon
pinch of fresh thyme
2 lb/900 g boiled potatoes, creamed with butter and milk and highly seasoned
¾ cup grated Cheddar cheese
salt and pepper
peas, to serve

**NUTRITION**
Calories *496*; Sugars *10 g*; Protein *38 g*; Carbohydrate *52 g*; Fat *17 g*; Saturates *9 g*

  moderate

 25 mins

45 mins

🍳 **COOK'S TIP**

Instead of Cheddar cheese, you could sprinkle fresh Jack Cheese, or even Toscana over the top, if available.

Low in fat and high in fiber, this colorful casserole makes a healthy, hearty, and utterly delicious one-pot meal.

# Rustic Chicken *and* Orange Pot

**SERVES 4**

8 skinless chicken drumsticks
1 tbsp whole-wheat flour
1 tbsp olive oil
2 medium red onions
1 garlic clove, crushed
1 tsp fennel seeds
1 bay leaf
finely grated rind and juice of 1 small orange
14 oz/400 g canned chopped tomatoes
14 oz/400 g canned cannellini or small navy beans, drained
salt and black pepper

*topping*

3 thick slices whole-wheat bread, crusts removed
2 tsp olive oil

1 Toss the chicken in the flour to coat evenly. Heat the oil in a nonstick pan. Add the chicken and cook over fairly high heat, turning frequently, until golden brown. Transfer to a large casserole.

2 Slice the red onions into thin wedges. Add to the pan and cook over medium heat for a few minutes until lightly browned. Stir in the garlic, then add the onions and garlic to the casserole.

3 Add the fennel seeds, bay leaf, orange rind and juice, tomatoes, and cannellini or small navy beans and season to taste with salt and pepper.

4 Cover tightly and cook in a preheated oven, 375°F/ 190°C, for 30–35 minutes until the chicken juices are clear and not pink when pierced through the thickest part with a skewer.

5 To make the topping, cut the bread into small dice and toss in the oil. Remove the lid from the casserole and sprinkle the bread cubes on top of the chicken. Bake for a further 15–20 minutes until the bread is golden and crisp. Serve immediately, straight from the casserole.

**NUTRITION**

Calories *345*; Sugars *6 g*; Protein *29 g*;
Carbohydrate *39 g*; Fat *10 g*; Saturates *2 g*

⭐⭐⭐     moderate
◔     5 mins
◷     1 hr

 **COOK'S TIP**

Choose beans which are canned in water with no added sugar or salt. Rinse and drain well before use.

Tender lean chicken is baked with pasta in a creamy low-fat sauce which contrasts well with the fennel and the sweetness of the raisins.

# Chicken Pasta Bake

1 Trim the fennel, reserving the green fronds, and slice the bulbs thinly.

2 Generously coat the onions in the lemon juice. Quarter the mushrooms.

3 Heat the oil in a large skillet and cook the fennel, onion, and mushrooms for 4–5 minutes, stirring, until just softened. Season well, transfer the mixture to a large bowl, and set aside.

4 Bring a pan of lightly salted water to a boil. Add the pasta, bring back to a boil, and cook for 8–10 minutes until tender, but still firm to the bite. Drain and mix the pasta with the vegetables.

5 Stir the raisins and chicken into the pasta mixture. Soften the soft cheese by beating it, then mix into the pasta and chicken—the heat from the pasta should make the cheese melt slightly.

6 Put the mixture into an ovenproof dish and place on a cookie sheet. Arrange slices of mozzarella cheese evenly over the top and sprinkle with the grated Parmesan cheese.

7 Bake in a preheated oven, 400°F/200°C, for 20–25 minutes until golden brown and the topping is bubbling. Garnish with chopped fennel fronds.

**SERVES 4**

2 bulbs fennel
2 red onions, shredded finely
1 tbsp lemon juice
4 oz/125 g white mushrooms
1 tbsp olive oil
2¼ cups dried penne
⅓ cup raisins
8 oz/225 g lean, boneless cooked chicken, skinned and shredded
13 oz/375 g low-fat soft cheese with garlic and herbs
4 oz/125 g low-fat mozzarella cheese, sliced thinly
scant ½ cup freshly grated Parmesan cheese
salt and pepper
chopped fennel fronds, to garnish

**NUTRITION**
Calories *643*; Sugars *20 g*; Protein *44 g*; Carbohydrate *64 g*; Fat *25 g*; Saturates *12 g*

⭐⭐   easy

15 mins

 40 mins

This aromatic chicken dish has a spicy Mexican kick. Chicken thighs have a wonderful flavor when cooked in this Latin American way.

# Chicken *and* Chili Bean Pot

### SERVES 4

2 tbsp all-purpose flour
1 tsp chili powder
8 chicken thighs or 4 chicken legs
3 tbsp vegetable oil
2 garlic cloves, crushed
1 large onion, chopped
1 green or red bell pepper, seeded and
    chopped
1¼ cups chicken bouillon
4 medium tomatoes, chopped
14 oz/400 g canned red kidney beans, rinsed
    and drained
2 tbsp tomato paste
salt and pepper

1 Mix together the flour, chili powder, and seasoning in a shallow dish. Rinse the chicken, then dip into the seasoned flour, turning to coat it on all sides.

2 Heat the oil in a skillet or pan, add the chicken, and brown for 3–4 minutes evenly on all sides.

3 Lift the chicken out of the pan with a draining spoon and drain.

4 Add the garlic, onion, and pepper to the pan and cook for 2–3 minutes, or until softened.

5 Add the bouillon, tomatoes, kidney beans, and tomato paste, stirring well. Bring to a boil, then return the chicken to the pan. Reduce the heat and simmer, covered, for about 30 minutes, or until the chicken is tender. Season and serve the bean pot at once while still hot.

### NUTRITION
Calories *333*; Sugars *10 g*; Protein *25 g*;
Carbohydrate *32 g*; Fat *13 g*; Saturates *2 g*

 easy

10 mins

40 mins

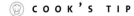 COOK'S TIP

For extra flavor, use sun-dried tomato paste instead of ordinary tomato paste.

This unusual dish, with its mixture of chicken and shellfish, is typically Spanish. The basis is *sofrito*: a slow-cooked mixture of onion and tomato in olive oil, with garlic and bell peppers.

# Spanish Chicken *with* Shrimp

1 Remove the skin from the chicken quarters. Heat the oil in a wide, heavy pan and sauté the chicken, turning occasionally until golden brown.

2 Using a sharp knife, seed and slice the bell pepper and peel and slice the onion. Add the bell pepper and onion to the pan and sauté gently to soften.

3 Add the garlic with the tomatoes, wine, and oregano. Season well with salt and pepper, then bring to a boil, cover and simmer gently for 45 minutes or until the chicken is tender and the juices run clear when the thickest part of the chicken is pierced with a skewer.

4 Thinly slice the chorizo and add to the pan together with the shrimp, then simmer for another 5 minutes. Adjust the seasoning and serve with rice.

**SERVES 4**

4 chicken quarters
1 tbsp olive oil
1 red bell pepper
1 medium onion
2 garlic cloves, crushed
14 oz canned chopped tomatoes
scant 1 cup dry white wine
4 tbsp chopped fresh oregano
salt and pepper
1 cup chorizo sausage
1 cup peeled shrimp
rice, to serve

**NUTRITION**
Calories *488*; Sugars *9 g*; Protein *69 g*;
Carbohydrate *10 g*; Fat *16 g*; Saturates *5 g*

easy

20 mins

1 hr 10 min

🍳 **COOK'S TIP**

Chorizo is a spicy Spanish sausage made with pork and a hot pepper such as cayenne or pimento. It is available from large stores and specialist butchers.

This famous dish is known throughout the world—it is perhaps the best known of all Italian risottos. This variation adds chicken.

# Chicken Risotto *à la* Milanese

### SERVES 4

½ cup butter
2 lb/900 g skinless boneless chicken, sliced thinly
1 large onion, chopped
1 lb/450 g risotto rice
2½ cups chicken bouillon
⅔ cup white wine
1 tsp crumbled saffron
salt and pepper
⅔ cup grated Parmesan cheese, to serve

1 Heat 4 tablespoons of the butter in a deep skillet and cook the chicken and onion until golden brown.

2 Add the rice, stir well, and cook over low heat for 15 minutes.

3 Heat the bouillon until boiling and gradually add to the rice. Add the white wine, saffron, salt and pepper to taste, and mix well. Simmer gently for 20 minutes, stirring occasionally, and adding more bouillon if necessary.

4 Set aside for 2–3 minutes and just before serving, add a little more bouillon and simmer for 10 minutes. Serve the risotto sprinkled with the grated Parmesan cheese and the remaining butter.

### NUTRITION

Calories *857*; Sugars *1 g*; Protein *57 g*; Carbohydrate *72 g*; Fat *38 g*; Saturates *21 g*

 easy

5 mins

1 hr 5 mins

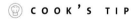 COOK'S TIP

A risotto should have moist but separate grains. Bouillon should be added a little at a time and only when the last addition has been completely absorbed.

If you prefer, long-grain rice can be used instead of risotto rice, but it will not give the traditional, creamy texture that is typical of Italian risottos.

# Golden Chicken Risotto

1 Heat oil and butter in a saucepan. Fry the leek and pepper for 1 minute, stir in the chicken and cook, stirring, until golden.

2 Stir in the risotto rice and cook for 2–3 minutes.

3 Stir in the saffron strands and salt and pepper. Add the chicken bouillon, a little at a time, then cover and cook over low heat, stirring occasionally, for about 20 minutes, or until the rice is tender and most of the liquid has been absorbed. Do not let the risotto dry out—add more bouillon if necessary.

4 Stir in the corn, peanuts, and freshly grated Parmesan cheese, then season with salt and pepper according to taste. Serve piping hot.

**SERVES 4**

2 tbsp sunflower oil
1 tbsp butter or margarine
1 leek, sliced thinly
1 large yellow bell pepper, diced
3 skinless, boneless chicken breasts, diced
1¾ cups risotto rice
strands of saffron
7 cups chicken bouillon
1 cup canned corn
½ cup unsalted peanuts, toasted
generous ½ cup Parmesan cheese, grated
salt and pepper

**NUTRITION**
Calories 701; Sugars 7 g; Protein 35 g; Carbohydrate 88 g; Fat 26 g; Saturates 8 g

   easy

10 mins

30 mins

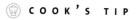 **COOK'S TIP**

Risottos can be frozen, before adding the Parmesan cheese, for up to 1 month, but remember to reheat this risotto thoroughly because it contains chicken.

This colorful dish will tempt the appetites of all the family. Children enjoy the fun shapes of the multicolored bell peppers.

# Harlequin Chicken

**SERVES 4**

10 skinless, boneless chicken thighs
1 onion
1 each red, green, and yellow bell peppers
1 tbsp sunflower oil
14 oz/400 g canned chopped tomatoes
2 tbsp chopped fresh parsley
pepper
whole-wheat bread and salad, to serve

1 Using a sharp knife, cut the chicken thighs into bite-size pieces.

2 Peel and thinly slice the onion. Halve and seed the peppers and cut into small diamond shapes.

3 Heat the sunflower oil in a shallow pan, then quickly fry the chicken and onion until golden.

4 Add the peppers and cook for 2–3 minutes, then stir in the tomatoes and chopped fresh parsley, and season with pepper.

5 Cover the pan tightly and simmer for approximately 15 minutes, or until the chicken and vegetables are tender. Remove from the pan and serve the Harlequin Chicken hot with whole-wheat bread and a green salad.

**NUTRITION**
Calories *183*; Sugars *8 g*; Protein *24 g*;
Carbohydrate *8 g*; Fat *6 g*; Saturates *1 g*

⭐ very easy

◔ 10 mins

🕐 25 mins

 **COOK'S TIP**

If you are making this dish for small children, the chicken can be finely chopped or ground first.

Small new potatoes are ideal for this recipe because they can be cooked whole. Cut larger potatoes in half or into chunks before using them.

# Chicken *and* Potato Casserole

**1** Heat the oil in a large skillet. Cook the chicken for 10 minutes, turning until browned. Transfer the chicken to a casserole dish using a draining spoon.

**2** Add the leek and garlic and cook for 2–3 minutes, stirring. Stir in the flour, cook for 1 minute and remove from the heat. Stir in the bouillon and wine.

**3** Return the skillet to the heat and bring to a boil. Stir in the carrots, corn, the potatoes, and bouquet garni, and season to taste. Transfer to the casserole dish.

**4** Cover and cook in a preheated oven, 350°F/180°C, for 1 hour.

**5** Remove the casserole to stir in the cream. Return to the oven, uncovered, and cook for 15 minutes. Remove the bouquet garni, season with salt and pepper, and serve with rice.

**SERVES 4**

2 tbsp vegetable oil
4 chicken portions (about 8 oz/225 g each)
2 leeks, sliced
1 garlic clove, crushed
4 tbsp all-purpose flour
3½ cups chicken bouillon
1¼ cups dry white wine
1 cup baby carrots, halved lengthwise
12 baby corn cobs, halved lengthwise
1 lb/450 g small new potatoes
1 bouquet garni
⅔ cup heavy cream
salt and pepper
rice, to serve

**NUTRITION**
Calories *856*; Sugars *7 g*; Protein *35 g*;
Carbohydrate *40 g*; Fat *58 g*; Saturates *26 g*

  moderate

15 mins

1 hr 35 mins

 **COOK'S TIP**

Use turkey fillets instead of the chicken, if preferred, and vary the vegetables according to those you have to hand.

Thai curries are traditionally very hot, and they make a little go a long way. The spiced juices are eaten with rice to "stretch" a small amount of meat.

# Green Chicken Curry

**SERVES 4**

6 boneless, skinless chicken thighs
1¾ cups coconut milk
2 garlic cloves, crushed
2 tbsp Thai fish sauce
2 tbsp Thai green curry paste
12 baby eggplants (or Thai pea eggplants)
3 green chiles, chopped finely
3 kaffir lime leaves, shredded
4 tbsp fresh chopped cilantro
salt and pepper
boiled rice, to serve

1  Cut the chicken into bite-size pieces. Pour the coconut milk into a large pan or wok over a high heat and bring to a boil.

2  Add the chicken, garlic, and fish sauce to the pan and bring back to a boil. Lower the heat and simmer for 30 minutes, or until the chicken is tender.

3  Remove the chicken from the mixture with a draining spoon. Set aside and keep warm.

4  Stir the green curry paste into the pan, then add the eggplants, chiles, and lime leaves and simmer for 5 minutes.

5  Return the chicken to the pan and bring to a boil. Adjust the seasoning to taste with salt and pepper, then stir in the cilantro. Serve the Green Chicken Curry with boiled rice.

**NUTRITION**
Calories *193*; Sugars *9 g*; Protein *22 g*;
Carbohydrate *9 g*; Fat *8 g*; Saturates *1 g*

⭐⭐    easy

🕐    10 mins

🕐    50 mins

 **COOK'S TIP**

Baby eggplants, or "pea eggplants", are traditionally used, but not always available outside the country. If you can't find them in an Asian food store, substitute chopped ordinary eggplant or a few green peas.

This tasty chicken dish combines warm spices and almonds and is spiked with anise.

# Fruity Garlic Curried Chicken

1 Heat the butter and 1 tablespoon of oil in a skillet, add the chicken pieces and cook for 5 minutes until golden. Transfer the chicken pieces to a plate and keep warm until required.

2 Combine the onion, gingerroot, garlic, almonds, red bell pepper, cumin, coriander, turmeric, cayenne pepper, and salt in a food processor or blender. Blend to form a smooth paste.

3 Heat the remaining oil in a large saucepan or deep skillet. Add the paste and fry for 10–12 minutes.

4 Add the chicken pieces, the water, star anise, lemon juice, and pepper. Cover, reduce the heat, and simmer gently for 25 minutes or until the chicken is tender, stirring a few times during cooking.

5 Transfer the chicken to a serving dish, sprinkle with the slivered almonds and serve with individual rice molds.

SERVES 4

2 tbsp butter
7 tbsp vegetable oil
4 skinless, boneless chicken breasts, cut into 2 x 1-inch/4 x 2-cm pieces
1 medium onion, chopped coarsely
1-inch/2-cm piece of fresh gingerroot
3 garlic cloves, peeled
¼ cup blanched almonds
1 large red bell pepper, chopped coarsely
1 tbsp ground cumin
2 tsp ground coriander
1 tsp ground turmeric
pinch cayenne pepper
½ tsp salt
⅔ cup water
3 star anise
2 tbsp lemon juice
pepper
slivered almonds, to garnish
rice, to serve

NUTRITION

Calories *421*; Sugars *5 g*; Protein *33 g*; Carbohydrate *7 g*; Fat *30 g*; Saturates *6 g*

easy

10 mins

45 mins

This is a simple version of a creamy and mildly spiced Indian pilau. There are many ingredients, but very little preparation needed for this dish.

# Golden Chicken Pilau

**SERVES 4**

4 tbsp butter
8 skinless, boneless chicken thighs, cut into large pieces
1 onion, sliced
1 tsp ground turmeric
1 tsp ground cinnamon
1½ cups long-grain rice
1¾ cups unsweetened yogurt
½ cup golden raisins
¾ cup chicken bouillon
1 tomato, chopped
2 tbsp chopped fresh cilantro or parsley
2 tbsp toasted coconut
salt and pepper
fresh cilantro, to garnish

1 Heat the butter in a heavy or nonstick skillet and fry the chicken with the onion for about 3 minutes.

2 Stir the turmeric, cinnamon, rice, and seasoning into the skillet and fry gently for 3 minutes.

3 Add the unsweetened yogurt, raisins, and chicken bouillon and mix well. Cover and simmer for 10 minutes, stirring occasionally until the rice is tender and all the chicken bouillon has been absorbed. Add more bouillon if the mixture starts to become too dry.

4 Stir in the chopped tomato and fresh cilantro or parsley. Season to taste.

5 Sprinkle the Golden Chicken Pilau with the toasted coconut and garnish with fresh cilantro to serve.

**NUTRITION**
Calories 581; Sugars 22 g; Protein 31 g;
Carbohydrate 73 g; Fat 19 g; Saturates 12 g

easy

10 mins

20 mins

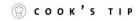

🍳 **COOK'S TIP**

Long-grain rice is the most widely available rice. Basmati, with its slender grains and aromatic flavor, is more expensive. All rice, especially basmati, should be washed thoroughly under cold running water before use.

Cooking in a single pot means that all of the flavors are retained. This is a substantial meal that needs only a salad and some crusty bread.

# Sage Chicken *and* Rice

1 Place the pieces of onion, garlic, celery, carrots, and sprigs of fresh sage in a large saucepan and pour in the chicken bouillon.

2 Bring the vegetable and herb mixture to a boil, then cover the pan and let simmer for 5 minutes.

3 Cut the chicken into 1-inch/2.5-cm cubes and stir into the pan with the vegetables. Cover the pan and continue to cook for another 5 minutes.

4 Stir in the mixed brown and wild rice and chopped tomatoes.

5 Add a dash of Tabasco sauce to taste and season well. Bring to a boil, then cover and simmer for 25 minutes.

6 Stir in the sliced zucchini and diced ham and continue to cook, uncovered, for another 10 minutes, stirring occasionally, until the rice is just tender.

7 Remove the sage sprigs and then discard them.

8 Garnish with sage leaves and serve with a salad and fresh crusty bread.

SERVES 4

1 large onion, chopped
1 garlic clove, crushed
2 celery stalks, sliced
2 carrots, diced
2 sprigs of fresh sage
1¼ cups chicken bouillon
12 oz/350 g skinless, boneless chicken breasts
generous 1 cup mixed brown and wild rice
14 oz/400 g canned chopped tomatoes
dash of Tabasco sauce
2 zucchini, trimmed and sliced thinly
½ cup diced lean ham
salt and pepper
fresh sage, to garnish

*to serve*
salad leaves
crusty bread

**NUTRITION**
Calories *247*; Sugars *5 g*; Protein *26 g*; Carbohydrate *25 g*; Fat *5 g*; Saturates *2 g*

easy

15 mins

45 mins

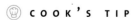 **COOK'S TIP**

If you do not have fresh sage, use 1 tsp of dried sage at Step 1.

Full of the flavors of fall, this combination of lean chicken, shallots, garlic, and fresh, juicy plums is a very fruity blend. Serve with bread to mop up the gravy.

# Chicken *and* Plum Casserole

### SERVES 4

2 slices lean bacon, rinds removed, trimmed and chopped
1 tbsp sunflower oil
1 lb skinless, boneless chicken thighs, cut into 4 equal strips
1 garlic clove, crushed
175g/6 oz shallots, halved
225g/8 oz plums, halved or quartered (if large) and pitted
1 tbsp light muscovado sugar
²⁄₃ cup dry sherry
2 tbsp plum sauce
2 cups Fresh Chicken Bouillon (see page 14)
2 tsp cornstarch mixed with 4 tsp cold water
2 tbsp chopped fresh parsley, to garnish
crusty bread, to serve

1 In a large, nonstick skillet, dry-fry the bacon for 2–3 minutes until the juices run out. Remove the bacon from the pan with a draining spoon, set aside, and keep warm.

2 In the same skillet, heat the oil and sauté the chicken with the garlic and shallots for 4–5 minutes, stirring occasionally, until well browned all over.

3 Return the bacon to the pan and stir in the plums, sugar, sherry, plum sauce, and bouillon. Bring to a boil and simmer for 20 minutes until the plums have softened and the chicken is cooked through.

4 Add the cornstarch mixture to the pan and cook, stirring, for another 2–3 minutes until thickened.

5 Spoon the casserole on to warm serving plates and garnish with chopped parsley. Serve with chunks of bread to mop up the fruity gravy.

### NUTRITION

Calories *325*; Sugars *11 g*; Protein *28 g*; Carbohydrate *16 g*; Fat *12 g*; Saturates *3 g*

 easy

15 mins

35 mins

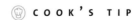

### COOK'S TIP

Chunks of lean turkey or pork would also go well with this combination of flavors. The cooking time will remain the same.

This succulent chicken is spiked with cayenne pepper and paprika, and finished off with a fruity, tangy sauce.

# Deviled Chicken

1 Mix the flour, cayenne pepper, and paprika together and use the mixture to coat the chicken.

2 Shake off any excess flour. Melt the butter in a saucepan and gently fry the chicken with the onion for 4 minutes.

3 Stir in the flour and spice mixture. Add the milk slowly until thickened.

4 Simmer gently over low heat until the sauce is smooth.

5 Add the applesauce and grapes and simmer gently for 20 minutes.

6 Transfer the chicken and deviled sauce to a serving dish and top with sour cream and a sprinkling of paprika.

### SERVES 2 – 3

¼ cup all-purpose flour
1 tbsp cayenne pepper
1 tsp paprika
12 oz/350 g skinless, boneless chicken, diced
2 tbsp butter
1 onion, chopped finely
2 cups milk, warmed
4 tbsp applesauce
1 cup green grapes
²/₃ cup sour cream
paprika, to garnish

### NUTRITION

Calories 455; Sugars 19 g; Protein 37 g; Carbohydrate 29 g; Fat 23 g; Saturates 14 g

 very easy

10 mins

35 mins

### COOK'S TIP

Add more paprika if desired—because it is quite a mild spice, you can add plenty without it being too overpowering.

This tasty dish combines the flavors of lime, peanut, coconut, and chile. You'll find coconut cream in most large food stores or delicatessens.

# Coconut Chicken *with* Lime

**SERVES 4**

⅔ cup hot chicken bouillon
⅓ cup creamed coconut
1 tbsp sunflower oil
8 skinless, boneless chicken thighs, cut into long, thin strips
1 small red chile, sliced thinly
4 scallions, sliced thinly
4 tbsp smooth or crunchy peanut butter
finely grated rind and juice of 1 lime
boiled rice, to serve

*to garnish*
1 fresh red chile
scallion "tassel"

1 Pour the chicken bouillon into a measuring cup or small bowl. Crumble the creamed coconut into the chicken bouillon and stir the mixture until the coconut dissolves.

2 Heat the oil in a preheated wok or large heavy pan.

3 Add the chicken strips and cook, stirring, until they turn a golden color.

4 Stir in the red chile and scallions and cook gently for a few minutes.

5 Add the peanut butter, coconut and chicken bouillon mixture, lime rind, and juice, and simmer, uncovered, for about 5 minutes, stirring frequently to prevent the mixture sticking to the bottom of the wok or pan.

6 Transfer the coconut chicken to a warm serving dish, garnish with the red chile and scallion tassel, and serve with boiled rice.

**NUTRITION**

Calories *348*; Sugars *2 g*; Protein *36 g*;
Carbohydrate *3 g*; Fat *21 g*; Saturates *8 g*

 moderate

5 mins

15 mins

**COOK'S TIP**

Serve jasmine rice with this spicy dish. It has a fragrant aroma that is well-suited to these flavors.

There are many versions of hotch–potch, all using fresh, local ingredients. Now, there is an endless variety of ingredients available all year, perfect for traditional one–pot cooking.

# Country Chicken Hotch-Potch

1 Remove the skin from the chicken quarters, if preferred.

2 Arrange a layer of potato slices in the bottom of a wide casserole. Season with salt and pepper, then add the thyme, rosemary, and bay leaves.

3 Top with the chicken quarters, then sprinkle with the diced bacon, onion, and carrots. Season well and arrange the remaining potato slices on top, overlapping slightly.

4 Pour over the beer, brush the potatoes with the melted butter, and cover the casserole with a lid.

5 Bake in a preheated oven, 300°F/150°c, for about 2 hours, uncovering for the last 30 minutes to let the potatoes brown. Serve hot.

**SERVES 4**

4 chicken quarters
6 medium potatoes, cut into
  ¼-inch/5-mm slices
salt and pepper
2 sprigs of fresh thyme
2 sprigs of fresh rosemary
2 bay leaves
1 cup diced, rindless, smoked bacon
1 large onion, chopped finely
1 cup sliced carrots
⅔ cup beer
2 tbsp melted butter

**NUTRITION**
Calories *499*; Sugars *6 g*; Protein *43 g*;
Carbohydrate *44 g*; Fat *17 g*; Saturates *8 g*

 easy

10 mins

2 hrs

##  COOK'S TIP

This dish is also delicious with stewing lamb, cut into chunks. You can add different vegetables depending on what is in season—try leeks and rutabaga for a slightly sweeter flavor.

This economical bake is a complete meal—its crusty, herb-flavored French bread topping mops up the tasty juices, and means there's no need to serve potatoes or rice separately.

# Chicken, Bean, *and* Celery Bake

**SERVES 4**

2 tbsp sunflower oil
4 chicken quarters
16 small whole onions, peeled
3 celery stalks, sliced
14 oz/400 g canned red kidney beans
4 medium tomatoes, quartered
scant 1 cup dry cider or bouillon
4 tbsp chopped fresh parsley
salt and pepper
1 tsp paprika
4 tbsp butter
12 slices French bread

1 Heat the oil in a flameproof casserole and sauté the chicken quarters two at a time until golden. Using a draining spoon, remove the chicken from the pan and set aside until required.

2 Add the onions and sauté, turning occasionally, until golden brown. Add the celery and sauté for 2–3 minutes. Return the chicken to the pan, then stir in the beans, tomatoes, cider, half the parsley, salt, and pepper. Sprinkle with the paprika.

3 Cover and cook in a preheated oven, 400°F/200°c, for 20–25 minutes, until the chicken juices run clear when pierced with a skewer.

4 Mix the remaining parsley with the butter and spread over the bread.

5 Uncover the casserole, arrange the bread slices so that they are overlapping on top, and bake for another 10–12 minutes, until golden and crisp.

**NUTRITION**
Calories 736; Sugars 11 g; Protein 50 g;
Carbohydrate 55 g; Fat 35 g; Saturates 13 g

easy

10 mins

1 hr

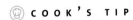 **COOK'S TIP**

For a more unusual Italian-tasting dish, spread the bread slices with pesto instead of the parsley butter.

A tasty way to make chicken joints go a long way, this hearty casserole, spiced with the warm, subtle flavor of ginger, is a good choice for a Halloween party.

# Jamaican Hotch–Potch

1 Heat the oil in a large flameproof casserole and sauté the chicken joints until golden, turning frequently.

2 Using a sharp knife, peel and slice the onion, peel and dice the squash or pumpkin, and seed and slice the bell pepper.

3 Drain any excess fat from the pan and add the prepared onion, pumpkin, and bell pepper. Gently sauté for a few minutes until lightly browned. Add the chopped gingerroot, tomatoes, chicken bouillon, and lentils. Season lightly with garlic salt and cayenne pepper.

4 Cover the casserole and place in a preheated oven, 375°F/190°c, for about 1 hour, until the vegetables are tender and the chicken juices run clear if pierced with a skewer.

5 Add the drained corn and cook for a further 5 minutes. Season to taste and serve with crusty bread.

SERVES 4

2 tsp sunflower oil
4 chicken drumsticks
4 chicken thighs
1 medium onion
1 lb 10 oz/750 g piece of squash or pumpkin, diced
1 green bell pepper, sliced
1-inch/2.5-cm piece of fresh gingerroot, chopped finely
14 oz/400 g canned chopped tomatoes
1¼ cups chicken bouillon
¼ cup split lentils, washed
garlic salt and cayenne pepper
¼ cup canned corn
crusty bread, to serve

NUTRITION

Calories 277; Sugars 6 g; Protein 33 g; Carbohydrate 22 g; Fat 7 g; Saturates 1 g

 COOK'S TIP

If squash or pumpkin is not available, rutabaga makes a good substitute.

⊕⊕        easy

        5 mins

        1 hr 15 mins

A colorful casserole packed with sunshine flavors from the Mediterranean. Sun–dried tomatoes add a wonderful richness and you need very few to make this dish really special.

# Rich Chicken Casserole

**SERVES 4**

8 chicken thighs
2 tbsp olive oil
1 medium red onion, sliced
2 garlic cloves, crushed
1 large red bell pepper, sliced thickly
thinly pared rind and juice of 1 small orange
½ cup chicken bouillon
14 oz/400 g canned chopped tomatoes
¼ cup sun-dried tomatoes, sliced thinly
1 tbsp chopped fresh thyme
½ cup pitted black olives
salt and pepper
sprigs of fresh thyme and orange rind, to garnish
crusty fresh bread, to serve

1 In a heavy-based or nonstick large skillet, sauté the chicken without fat over a fairly high heat, turning occasionally until golden brown. Using a draining spoon, drain off any excess fat from the chicken and transfer to a flameproof casserole.

2 Sauté the onion, garlic, and bell pepper in the pan over moderate heat for 3–4 minutes. Transfer to the casserole.

3 Add the orange peel and juice, chicken bouillon, canned tomatoes, and sun-dried tomatoes and stir to combine.

4 Bring to a boil then cover the casserole with a lid and simmer very gently over low heat for about 1 hour, stirring occasionally. Add the chopped thyme and pitted black olives, then adjust the seasoning with salt and pepper.

5 Scatter orange rind and thyme over the casserole to garnish, and serve with crusty bread.

**NUTRITION**
Calories *260*; Sugars *8 g*; Protein *32 g*; Carbohydrate *8 g*; Fat *11 g*; Saturates *2 g*

moderate

5 mins

1 hr 15 mins

🍴 **COOK'S TIP**

Sun–dried tomatoes have a dense texture and concentrated taste, and add intense flavor to slow–cooking casseroles.

This is a good way to use up leftover rice. Use fresh or canned sweet pink grapefruit for an interesting alternative to the orange.

# Orange Turkey *with* Rice

1 Heat the oil in a large skillet and cook the onion and turkey, stirring, for 4–5 minutes until lightly browned.

2 Pour in the orange juice and add the bay leaf and seasoning. Bring to a boil and simmer for 10 minutes.

3 Meanwhile, bring a large pan of water to a boil and cook the broccoli florets, covered, for 2 minutes. Add the diced zucchini, then bring back to a boil. Cover and cook for another 3 minutes. Drain and set aside.

4 Using a sharp knife, peel off the skin and white pith from the orange. Slice down the orange to make thin circular slices, then halve each slice.

5 Stir the broccoli, zucchini, rice, and orange slices into the turkey mixture. Gently mix together and season, then heat through for a further 3–4 minutes, or until the mixture is piping hot.

6 Transfer the turkey rice to warm serving plates and garnish with black olives and shredded basil leaves. Serve with a fresh tomato and onion salad.

**SERVES 4**

1 tbsp olive oil
1 medium onion, chopped
1 lb/450 g skinless lean turkey (such as fillet), cut into thin strips
1¼ cups unsweetened orange juice
1 bay leaf
3 cups small broccoli florets
1 large zucchini, diced
1 large orange
6 cups cooked brown rice
salt and pepper
tomato and onion salad, to serve

*to garnish*
9–10 pitted black olives in brine, drained and quartered
shredded basil leaves

**NUTRITION**
Calories *337*; Sugars *12 g*; Protein *32 g*; Carbohydrate *40 g*; Fat *7 g*; Saturates *1 g*

⭐⭐⭐⭐ challenging
🕐 30 mins
🕐 40 mins

# Vegetables

Nutritionists tell us that we should eat more vegetables, but it isn't always easy to persuade the family to eat up their greens, especially if they are sitting in an unappetizing heap on the side of the plate. This chapter provides the answer with a spectacular collection of mouthwatering vegetable dishes—soups, bakes, risottos, casseroles, and curries. Beans, peas, lentils, broccoli, cauliflower, mushrooms, bell peppers, onions, zucchini, tomatoes, even the humble potato, take a starring role and are combined with each other for a colorful, melt-in-the-mouth medley or with other ingredients, such as pasta, to satisfy even the hungriest appetite. A vegetarian main course is an easy way to ring the changes in the weekly menu and, because vegetables tend to cook quite quickly, it will give the family cook a welcome break. From Mushroom and Cheese Risotto to Coconut Vegetable Curry, vegetables have never looked—or tasted—so good.

A slightly hot and spicy Indian flavor is given to this soup with the use of garam masala, chile, cumin, and cilantro.

# Indian Potato *and* Pea Soup

**SERVES 4**

2 tbsp vegetable oil
1¼ cups diced mealy potatoes
1 large onion, chopped
2 garlic cloves, crushed
1 tsp garam masala
1 tsp ground coriander
1 tsp ground cumin
3¾ cups vegetable bouillon
1 fresh red chile, chopped
¾ cup frozen peas
4 tbsp low-fat plain yogurt
salt and pepper
chopped fresh cilantro, to garnish
warm bread, to serve

1 Heat the vegetable oil in a large pan and add the potatoes, onion, and garlic. Sauté gently for about 5 minutes, stirring constantly.

2 Add the garam masala, ground coriander, and ground cumin, and cook for 1 minute, stirring all the time.

3 Stir in the vegetable bouillon and red chile and bring the mixture to a boil. Reduce the heat, cover, and simmer for 20 minutes, until the potatoes begin to break down.

4 Add the peas and cook for another 5 minutes. Stir in the yogurt and season with salt and pepper to taste.

5 Pour into warm soup bowls. Garnish with the cilantro and serve hot with warm bread.

**NUTRITION**
Calories *153*; Sugars *8 g*; Protein *6 g*;
Carbohydrate *18 g*; Fat *6 g*; Saturates *1 g*

 very easy

 15 mins

 30 mins

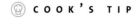 **COOK'S TIP**

For slightly less heat, seed the chile before adding it to the soup. Always wash your hands after handling chiles because they contain volatile oils that can irritate the skin and make your eyes burn if you touch your face.

This hearty soup is wonderful made in the middle of winter with fresh seasonal vegetables. Use a really well-flavored sharp colby cheese.

# Cheese *and* Vegetable Chowder

1 Melt the butter in a large, heavy pan over medium-low heat. Add the onion, leek, and garlic. Cover and cook for about 5 minutes, stirring frequently, until the vegetables start to soften.

2 Stir the flour into the vegetables and continue cooking for 2 minutes. Add a little of the bouillon and stir well, scraping the bottom of the pan to mix in the flour. Bring to a boil, stirring, and slowly stir in the rest of the bouillon.

3 Add the carrots, celery, turnip, potato, thyme, and bay leaf. Reduce the heat, cover, and cook gently for about 35 minutes, stirring occasionally, until the vegetables are tender. Remove the bay leaf and the thyme sprigs.

4 Stir the light cream into the soup and simmer over very low heat for 5 minutes. Add the grated cheese a handful at a time, stirring constantly for 1 minute after each addition, to make sure it is completely melted.

5 Taste the soup, adding salt if needed, and pepper to taste.

6 Serve immediately in warm bowls, garnished with chopped fresh parsley.

**SERVES 4**

2 tbsp butter
1 large onion, chopped finely
1 large leek, split lengthwise and sliced thinly
1–2 garlic cloves, crushed
6 tbsp all-purpose flour
5 cups vegetable bouillon
3 carrots, diced finely
2 stalks celery, diced finely
1 turnip, diced finely
1 large potato, diced finely
3–4 sprigs of fresh thyme, or ⅛ tsp dried thyme
1 bay leaf
1½ cups light cream
2¼ cups grated sharp colby cheese
fresh chopped parsley, to garnish
salt and pepper

**NUTRITION**
Calories *669*; Sugars *13 g*; Protein *26 g*; Carbohydrate *33 g*; Fat *49 g*; Saturates *30 g*

 moderate

15 mins

20 mins

Mediterranean vegetables, roasted in olive oil and flavored with thyme, are the basis for this soup.

# Roasted Vegetable Soup

**SERVES 6**

2–3 tbsp olive oil

1 ½ lb/675 g ripe tomatoes, skinned, cored, and halved

3 large yellow bell peppers, halved, cored, and seeded

3 zucchini, halved lengthwise

1 small eggplant, halved lengthwise

4 garlic cloves, halved

2 onions, cut into eighths

pinch of dried thyme

4 cups vegetable bouillon

½ cup light cream

salt and pepper

shredded basil leaves, to garnish

1 Brush a large shallow baking dish with olive oil. Laying them cut-side down, arrange the tomatoes, bell peppers, zucchini, and eggplant in one layer (use two dishes, if necessary). Tuck the garlic cloves and onion pieces into the gaps and drizzle the vegetables with olive oil. Season lightly with salt and pepper and sprinkle with the thyme.

2 Place in a preheated oven at 375°F/190°C and bake the vegetables, uncovered, for 30–35 minutes, or until they are soft and browned around the edges. Let cool, then scrape out the eggplant flesh and skin the bell peppers.

3 Working in batches, put the eggplant and bell pepper flesh, together with the zucchini, into a food processor and chop to the consistency of salsa; do not purée. Alternatively, place in a bowl and chop together with a knife.

4 Combine the bouillon and chopped vegetable mixture in a pan and simmer over medium heat for about 20–30 minutes until all the vegetables are tender and the flavors have completely blended.

5 Stir the cream into the soup and simmer over low heat for about 5 minutes, stirring occasionally, until hot. Taste and adjust the seasoning, if necessary. Ladle the soup into warm bowls, garnish with basil, and serve.

**NUTRITION**

Calories 163; Sugars 13 g; Protein 5 g; Carbohydrate 15 g; Fat 10 g; Saturates 3 g

moderate

15 mins

1 hr 10 mins

This thick, satisfying blend of beans and diced vegetables in a rich red wine and tomato bouillon makes an ideal simple supper.

# Tuscan Bean Soup

1 Place the prepared onion, garlic, celery, and carrot in a large saucepan. Stir in the tomatoes, red wine, vegetable bouillon, and oregano.

2 Bring the vegetable mixture to a boil, then cover and let simmer for 15 minutes. Stir the beans and zucchini into the mixture, and continue to cook, uncovered, for another 5 minutes.

3 Add the tomato paste to the mixture and season well with salt and pepper to taste. Then heat through, stirring occasionally, for another 2–3 minutes, but do not let the mixture boil again.

4 Ladle the soup into warm bowls and serve with a spoonful of pesto on each portion and accompanied with chunks of crusty bread.

SERVES 4

1 medium onion, chopped
1 garlic clove, chopped finely
2 celery stalks, sliced
1 large carrot, diced
14 oz/400 g canned chopped tomatoes
²/₃ cup Italian dry red wine
5 cups fresh vegetable bouillon
1 tsp dried oregano
1½ cups canned mixed beans and pulses
2 medium zucchini, diced
1 tbsp tomato paste
salt and pepper

*to serve*
pesto (see page 99)
crusty bread

**NUTRITION**
Calories *192*; Sugars *10 g*; Protein *10 g*;
Carbohydrate *23 g*; Fat *5 g*; Saturates *1 g*

 moderate

15 mins

35 mins

🍳 **COOK'S TIP**

For a more substantial soup, add 12 oz/350 g diced lean cooked chicken or turkey with the beans and zucchini at Step 2.

This soup is best made with white onions, which have a milder flavor than the more usual brown variety. If you cannot get hold of them, use large Bermuda onions.

# Tuscan Onion Soup

## SERVES 4

½ cup pancetta, diced
1 tbsp olive oil
4 large white onions, sliced thinly in rings
3 garlic cloves, chopped
3¾ cups hot chicken or ham bouillon
4 slices ciabatta or other Italian bread
3 tbsp butter
¾ cup coarsely grated Gruyère or Cheddar
salt and pepper

1 Dry-fry the pancetta in a large pan for 3–4 minutes, or until it begins to brown. Remove the pancetta from the pan and set aside until required.

2 Add the oil to the pan and cook the onions and garlic over high heat for 4 minutes. Reduce the heat, then cover and cook for 15 minutes, or until lightly caramelized.

3 Add the bouillon to the pan and bring to a boil. Reduce the heat and leave the mixture to simmer, covered, for about 10 minutes.

4 Toast the slices of ciabatta on both sides, under a preheated broiler, for 2–3 minutes, or until golden. Spread the ciabatta with butter and top with the Gruyère or Cheddar cheese. Cut the bread into bite-size pieces.

5 Add the reserved pancetta to the soup and season to taste with salt and pepper. Pour into 4 soup bowls and top with the toasted bread.

## NUTRITION

Calories 390; Sugars 0g; Protein 9g;
Carbohydrate 15 g; Fat 33 g; Saturates 14 g

⭐ very easy
🕐 5–10 mins
🕐 40–45 mins

 **COOK'S TIP**

Pancetta is similar to bacon, but it is air- and salt-cured for about 6 months. It is available from most delicatessens and some large supermarkets. If you cannot obtain pancetta, use unsmoked bacon instead.

A *minestra* is a soup cooked with pasta; farfalline, a small bow-shaped variety, is used in this case. Served with lentils, this hearty soup is a meal in itself.

# Brown Lentil Soup *with* Pasta

1 Place the bacon in a large skillet together with the onions, garlic, and celery. Dry-fry for 4–5 minutes, stirring, until the onion is tender and the bacon is just beginning to brown.

2 Add the farfalline or spaghetti pieces to the skillet and cook, stirring, for about 1 minute to coat the pasta well in the oil.

3 Add the lentils and the bouillon and bring to a boil. Reduce the heat and leave to simmer for 12–15 minutes, or until the pasta is tender.

4 Remove the skillet from the heat and stir in the chopped fresh mint.

5 Transfer the soup to warm soup bowls and serve immediately.

**SERVES 4**

4 bacon slices, cut into small squares
1 onion, chopped
2 garlic cloves, crushed
2 celery stalks, chopped
¼ cup farfalline or spaghetti, broken into small pieces
2 cups canned brown lentils, drained
5 cups hot ham or vegetable bouillon
2 tbsp chopped fresh mint

**NUTRITION**
Calories *225*; Sugars *1 g*; Protein *13 g*; Carbohydrate *27 g*; Fat *8 g*; Saturates *3 g*

 easy
 5 mins
 25 mins

**COOK'S TIP**

If you prefer to use dried lentils, add the bouillon before the pasta and cook for 1–1¼ hours, until the lentils are tender. Add the pasta and cook for an additional 12–15 minutes.

Packed with the flavor of garlic, this soup makes a filling supper dish when served with crusty bread and a crisp salad.

# Lentil *and* Pasta Soup

### SERVES 4

1 tbsp olive oil
1 medium onion, chopped
4 garlic cloves, chopped finely
1½ cups carrot, sliced
1 stalk celery, sliced
1½ cups split red lentils, washed
2½ cups vegetable bouillon
3 cups boiling water
1½ cups pasta shapes
⅔ cups low-fat unsweetened yogurt, plus extra to serve
salt and pepper
2 tbsp chopped fresh parsley, to garnish

1 Heat the olive oil in a large pan and sauté the prepared onion, garlic, carrot, and celery, stirring gently, for about 5 minutes or until they begin to soften.

2 Add the lentils, bouillon, and boiling water. Season well, stir, and bring back to a boil. Simmer, uncovered, for 15 minutes until the lentils are completely tender. Let cool for 10 minutes.

3 Meanwhile, bring another pan of water to a boil and cook the pasta according to the instructions on the package. Drain well and set aside.

4 Place the soup in a blender and process until smooth. Return to a pan and add the pasta. Bring back to a simmer and heat for 2–3 minutes until piping hot. Remove from the heat and stir in the unsweetened yogurt. Adjust the seasoning if necessary.

5 Serve sprinkled with freshly ground black pepper and chopped parsley and with extra yogurt if wished.

### NUTRITION

Calories *390*; Sugars *12 g*; Protein *20 g*; Carbohydrate *71 g*; Fat *5 g*; Saturates *1 g*

easy

15 mins

55 mins

### 👨‍🍳 COOK'S TIP

Avoid boiling the soup once the yogurt has been added. Otherwise it will separate and become watery, spoiling the appearance of the soup.

This soup takes advantage of summer vegetables bursting with flavor. If you find fresh small cannellini or other fresh beans, be sure to use them.

# Green Vegetable Soup

1 Heat the oil in a large pan. Cook the onion and leek over low heat, stirring occasionally, for 5 minutes. Add the celery, carrot, and garlic, cover, and cook for another 5 minutes.

2 Add the water, potato, parsnip, kohlrabi or turnip, and green beans. Bring to a boil, reduce the heat, cover, and simmer for 5 minutes.

3 Add the peas, zucchini, and small cannellini beans and season to taste. Cover and simmer for about 25 minutes until all the vegetables are tender.

4 Meanwhile, make the pesto. Put all the ingredients in a food processor and process until smooth, scraping down the sides as necessary. Alternatively, pound together using a pestle and mortar.

5 Add the spinach to the soup and simmer for 5 minutes. Stir in a spoonful of the pesto. Ladle into bowls and pass the remaining pesto separately.

**SERVES 6**

1 tbsp olive oil
1 onion, chopped finely
1 large leek, split and sliced thinly
1 celery stalk, sliced thinly
1 carrot, quartered and sliced thinly
1 garlic clove, chopped finely
6¼ cups water
1 potato, diced
1 parsnip, diced finely
1 small kohlrabi or turnip, diced
1 cup green beans, cut in small pieces
1¼ cups fresh or frozen peas
2 small zucchini, sliced
1½ cups canned small cannellini beans, drained and rinsed
2 firmly packed cups shredded spinach leaves, cut into ribbons
salt and pepper

*pesto*

1 large garlic clove, very chopped finely
½ cup fresh basil leaves
1 cup freshly grated Parmesan cheese
4 tbsp extra virgin olive oil

**NUTRITION**
Calories *260*; Sugars *7 g*; Protein *12 g*;
Carbohydrate *21 g*; Fat *15 g*; Saturates *4 g*

easy

20 mins

50 mins

This simple recipe uses the sweet potato with its distinctive flavor and color, combined with a hint of orange and cilantro.

# Sweet Potato *and* Onion Soup

**SERVES 4**

2 tbsp vegetable oil
2 lb/900 g sweet potatoes, diced
1 carrot, diced
2 onions, sliced
2 garlic cloves, crushed
2½ cups vegetable bouillon
1¼ cups unsweetened orange juice
1 cup low-fat plain yogurt
2 tbsp chopped fresh cilantro
salt and pepper

*to garnish*
sprigs of fresh cilantro
strips of orange rind

1 Heat the vegetable oil in a large, heavy pan and add the sweet potatoes, carrot, onions, and garlic. Sauté the vegetables over low heat, stirring constantly for 5 minutes until softened.

2 Pour in the vegetable bouillon and orange juice and bring to a boil.

3 Reduce the heat to a simmer, cover the pan, and cook the vegetables for 20 minutes or until the sweet potatoes and carrot are tender.

4 Transfer the mixture to a food processor or blender, in batches, and process for 1 minute until puréed. Return the purée to the rinsed-out pan.

5 Stir in the yogurt and cilantro and season to taste with salt and pepper.

6 Serve in warm bowls and garnish with cilantro sprigs and orange rind.

**NUTRITION**
Calories *320*; Sugars *26 g*; Protein *7 g*;
Carbohydrate *62 g*; Fat *7 g*; Saturates *1 g*

 very easy

15 mins

30 mins

🍲 **COOK'S TIP**

This soup can be chilled before serving, if preferred. If chilling, stir the yogurt into the dish just before serving. Serve in chilled bowls.

This soup makes an excellent winter lunch served with warm crusty bread and a slice of cheese.

# Navy Bean *and* Pasta Soup

1 Put the navy beans in a large saucepan, add sufficient cold water to cover and bring to a boil. Boil vigorously over high heat for 15 minutes. Drain the beans and keep warm.

2 Heat the oil in a pan over medium heat and fry the onions for 2–3 minutes or until they are just beginning to change color. Stir in the garlic and cook for 1 minute. Stir in the tomatoes, oregano, and tomato paste.

3 Add the water and the beans to the pan. Bring to a boil, cover, then lower the heat and simmer for about 45 minutes, or until the beans are tender.

4 Add the pasta to the pan and season to taste with salt and pepper. Stir in the sun-dried tomatoes, bring back to a boil, partly cover, and simmer for 10 minutes, or until the pasta is tender, but still firm to the bite.

5 Stir the cilantro or parsley into the soup. Ladle the soup into a warm tureen, sprinkle over the Parmesan cheese and serve immediately.

serves 4

1⅓ cups navy beans, soaked for 3 hours in cold water and drained
4 tbsp olive oil
2 large onions, sliced
3 garlic cloves, chopped
400 g/14 oz canned chopped tomatoes
1 tsp dried oregano
1 tsp tomato paste
3½ cups water
¾ cup dried fusilli or conchigliette
1 cup sun-dried tomatoes, drained and sliced thinly
1 tbsp chopped fresh cilantro or flatleaf parsley
salt and pepper
2 tbsp Parmesan cheese shavings, to serve

**NUTRITION**
Calories *519*; Sugars *13 g*; Protein *20 g*;
Carbohydrate *67 g*; Fat *21 g*; Saturates *3 g*

 easy

3 hrs 10 mins

1 hrs 15 mins

🍳 **COOK'S TIP**

If preferred, place the beans in a pan of cold water and bring to a boil. Remove from the heat and leave the beans to cool in the water. Drain and rinse the beans before using.

This soup is a delicious
and filling treat on cold
winter evenings.

# Noodle Soup

**SERVES 4**

3 slices smoked, rindless bacon, diced

1 large onion, chopped

1 tbsp butter

2½ cups dried peas, soaked in cold water for
    2 hours and drained

10 cups chicken bouillon

8 oz dried egg noodles

⅝ cup heavy cream

salt and pepper

chopped fresh parsley, to garnish

Parmesan cheese croutons (see Cook's Tip,
    right), to serve

1 Put the bacon, onion, and butter into a large pan and cook over a low heat
for about 6 minutes.

2 Add the peas and the chicken bouillon to the pan and bring to a boil. Season
lightly with salt and pepper, cover and simmer for 1½ hours.

3 Add the egg noodles to the pan and simmer for an additional 15 minutes.

4 Pour in the cream and blend thoroughly. Transfer to a warm tureen, garnish
with parsley, top with Parmesan cheese croutons (see Cook's Tip ), and serve.

**NUTRITION**

Calories *835*; Sugars *8 g*; Protein *37 g*;
Carbohydrate *105 g*; Fat *33 g*; Saturates *16 g*

 easy

2 hrs 10 mins

1 hr 50 mins

 **COOK'S TIP**

To make Parmesan cheese croutons, cut a French stick into slices. Coat lightly
with olive oil and sprinkle with Parmesan. Broil for about 30 seconds.

This soup highlights the rich flavor of healthy green broccoli. To make a smooth soup, purée the cooked ingredients before serving.

# Broccoli Soup

1 Cut off the stems from the broccoli florets. Peel the large stems. Chop all the stems into small pieces.

2 Heat the butter and oil in a large pan over medium heat and add the onion, leek, and carrot. Cook the vegetable mixture for 3–4 minutes, stirring frequently, until the onion is soft.

3 Add the broccoli stems, rice, water, bay leaf, and a pinch of salt. Bring just to a boil and reduce the heat to low. Cover and simmer for 15 minutes. Add the broccoli florets and continue cooking, covered, for 15–20 minutes, or until the rice and vegetables are tender. Remove the bay leaf.

4 Season the soup with grated nutmeg, black pepper, and, if needed, more salt. Stir in the cream and cream cheese. Simmer over low heat for a few minutes, or until heated through, stirring occasionally. Adjust the seasoning, if needed. Ladle into warm bowls and serve sprinkled with croutons.

**SERVES 4**

3½ cups broccoli (florets)
2 tsp butter
1 tsp oil
1 onion, chopped finely
1 leek, sliced thinly
1 small carrot, chopped finely
3 tbsp white rice
3½ cups water
1 bay leaf
freshly grated nutmeg
4 tbsp heavy cream
3½ oz/100 g cream cheese
salt and pepper
croutons, to serve (see Cook's Tip)

**NUTRITION**
Calories *384*; Sugars *7 g*; Protein *8 g*;
Carbohydrate *21 g*; Fat *30 g*; Saturates *18 g*

★★★   moderate

15 mins

50 mins

 **COOK'S TIP**

To make croutons, remove the crusts from thick slices of bread, then cut the bread into dice. Fry in vegetable oil, stirring constantly, until evenly browned, then drain on paper towels.

Mild red chili powder and pan-browned garlic give flavor to this simple, vegetable soup. Quick to make, it's ideal for a light lunch.

# Spicy Zucchini Soup

**SERVES 4**

2 tbsp vegetable oil
4 garlic cloves, sliced thinly
1–2 tbsp mild red chili powder
$\frac{1}{4}$–$\frac{1}{2}$ tsp ground cumin
6$\frac{3}{4}$ cups chicken, vegetable, or beef bouillon
2 zucchini, cut into bite-size chunks
4 tbsp long-grain rice
salt and pepper
sprigs of fresh oregano, to garnish
lime wedges, to serve (optional)

1 Heat the oil in a heavy-based pan, add the garlic, and cook, stirring frequently, for about 2 minutes until softened and just beginning to change color. Stir in the chili powder and cumin and cook over medium-low heat, stirring constantly, for a minute.

2 Stir in the bouillon, zucchini, and rice, then cook over medium-high heat for about 10 minutes until the zucchini are just tender and the rice is cooked through. Season the soup to taste with salt and pepper.

3 Ladle into warmed bowls, garnish with oregano, and serve with lime wedges.

**NUTRITION**
Calories *98*; Sugars *1 g*; Protein *2 g*;
Carbohydrate *8 g*; Fat *7 g*; Saturates *1 g*

 very easy

 5 mins

15 mins

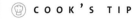 **COOK'S TIP**

Instead of rice, use tiny pasta, such as orzo, or very thin pasta known as fideo. Use yellow summer squash instead of the zucchini and add cooked pinto beans in place of the rice. Diced tomatoes also make a tasty addition.

Crisp tortilla chips act as croutons in this hearty vegetable soup which is found throughout Mexico. Add cheese to melt in, if you wish.

# Mexican Vegetable Soup

1 Heat the oil in a heavy-based pan. Add the onion and garlic and cook for a few minutes until softened, then sprinkle in the cumin and chili powder. Stir in the carrot, potato, tomatoes, zucchini, and cabbage and cook, stirring occasionally, for 2 minutes.

2 Pour in the bouillon. Cover and cook over medium heat for about 20 minutes until the vegetables are tender.

3 Add extra water if necessary, then stir in the corn and green beans, and cook for another 5–10 minutes or until the beans are tender. Season with salt and pepper to taste, bearing in mind that the tortilla chips may be salty.

4 Ladle the soup into soup bowls and sprinkle each portion with fresh cilantro. Top with a spoon of salsa, then add a handful of tortilla chips.

SERVES  4

2 tbsp vegetable or extra virgin olive oil
1 onion, chopped finely
4 garlic cloves, chopped finely
¼–½ tsp ground cumin
2–3 tsp mild chili powder
1 carrot, sliced
1 potato, diced
1½ cups diced fresh or canned tomatoes
1 zucchini, diced
¼ small cabbage, shredded
4 cups vegetable or chicken bouillon or water
the kernels from 1-2 corn cobs or 1 cup canned corn
about 10 green beans, cut into bite-size lengths
salt and pepper

*to serve*
4–6 tbsp chopped fresh cilantro
salsa of your choice or chopped fresh chile, to taste
tortilla chips

## NUTRITION
Calories *201*; Sugars *9 g*; Protein *6 g*; Carbohydrate *27 g*; Fat *9 g*; Saturates *1 g*

⭐⭐ easy

10 mins

 40 mins

This is a well-known method of cooking vegetables and is perfect with shallots or onions, served with a crisp salad.

# Onions *à la* Grecque

**SERVES 4**

1 lb/450 g shallots
3 tbsp olive oil
3 tbsp honey
2 tbsp garlic wine vinegar
3 tbsp dry white wine
1 tbsp tomato paste
2 celery stalks, sliced
2 tomatoes, seeded and chopped
salt and pepper
chopped celery leaves, to garnish

1 Peel the shallots. Heat the oil in a large pan, add the shallots and cook, stirring, for 3–5 minutes, or until they begin to brown.

2 Add the honey and cook over high heat for another 30 seconds, then add the garlic wine vinegar and dry white wine, stirring well.

3 Stir in the tomato paste, the celery, and the tomatoes, and bring the mixture to a boil. Cook over high heat for 5–6 minutes. Season to taste with salt and pepper and let cool slightly.

4 Garnish with chopped celery leaves and serve warm. Alternatively, chill in the refrigerator before serving.

**NUTRITION**
Calories *200*; Sugars *26 g*; Protein *2 g*;
Carbohydrate *28 g*; Fat *9 g*; Saturates *1 g*

　very easy

🕐　10 mins

🕐　15 mins

Poppy seeds add texture and flavor to this recipe and counteract the slightly sweet flavor of the carrots.

# Carrot *and* Orange Bake

1 Cook the carrots and leek in a pan of boiling lightly salted water for 5–6 minutes. Drain well and transfer to a shallow ovenproof dish until required.

2 Mix together the orange juice, honey, garlic, allspice, and thyme and pour the mixture over the vegetables. Season with salt and pepper to taste.

3 Cover the dish and cook in a preheated oven, 350°F/180°C, for about 30 minutes, or until all the vegetables are tender.

4 Remove the lid and sprinkle with poppy seeds. Transfer the bake to a warmed serving dish, garnish with the fresh thyme sprigs and orange rind strips, and serve immediately.

**SERVES 4**

1½ lb/675 g carrots, cut into thin strips
1 leek, sliced
1¼ cups fresh orange juice
2 tbsp clear honey
1 garlic clove, crushed
1 tsp allspice
2 tsp chopped thyme
1 tbsp poppy seeds
salt and pepper

*to garnish*
sprigs of fresh thyme
strips of orange rind

## COOK'S TIP

Lemon or lime juice could be used instead of the orange juice, if you prefer. Garnish with lemon or lime rind.

**NUTRITION**
Calories 138; Sugars 31 g; Protein 2 g;
Carbohydrate 32 g; Fat 1 g; Saturates 0.2 g

  easy

  20 mins

  40 mins

This is a quick one-pan dish which is ideal for a snack. Packed with color and flavor, it is very versatile, because you can add other vegetables.

# Potato *and* Mushroom Hash

## SERVES 4

1½ lb/675 g potatoes, cubed
1 tbsp olive oil
2 garlic cloves, crushed
1 green bell pepper, seeded and cubed
1 yellow bell pepper, seeded and cubed
3 tomatoes, diced
1 cup white mushrooms, halved
1 tbsp Worcestershire sauce
2 tbsp chopped basil
salt and pepper
sprigs of basil, to garnish
warm crusty bread, to serve

1 Cook the potatoes in a pan of boiling salted water for 7–8 minutes. Drain well and reserve.

2 Heat the olive oil in a large, heavy-based skillet. Add the potatoes and cook, stirring constantly, for 8–10 minutes, until browned.

3 Add the garlic and bell peppers and cook, stirring frequently, for 2–3 minutes.

4 Stir the tomatoes and mushrooms into the pan and cook, stirring frequently, for 5–6 minutes.

5 Stir in the Worcestershire sauce and basil and season to taste with salt and pepper. Transfer to a warm serving dish. Garnish with basil sprigs and serve with warm crusty bread.

## NUTRITION

Calories *182*; Sugars *6 g*; Protein *5 g*;
Carbohydrate *34 g*; Fat *4 g*; Saturates *0.5 g*

easy

5 mins

30 mins

🍴 **COOK'S TIP**

Most brands of Worcestershire sauce contain anchovies, so if you are vegetarian, check the label to make sure you choose a vegetarian variety.

This dish contains many Greek flavors such as lemon, garlic, oregano, and olives, for a really flavorful recipe.

# Greek Beans

1 Put the navy beans in a flameproof casserole dish.

2 Add the olive oil and crushed garlic and cook over gentle heat, stirring occasionally, for 4–5 minutes.

3 Stir in the vegetable bouillon, bay leaf, oregano, tomato paste, lemon juice, and red onion.

4 Cover the casserole and simmer for about 1 hour or until the sauce has thickened.

5 Stir in the black olives, and season with salt and pepper to taste. The beans are delicious served warm or cold.

**SERVES 4**

2 cups canned navy beans, drained
1 tbsp olive oil
3 garlic cloves, crushed
1¾ cups vegetable bouillon
1 bay leaf
2 sprigs oregano
1 tbsp tomato paste
juice of 1 lemon
1 small red onion, chopped
¼ cup pitted black olives, halved
salt and pepper

**NUTRITION**
Calories *115*; Sugars *4 g*; Protein *6 g*; Carbohydrate *15 g*; Fat *4 g*; Saturates *0.6 g*

 very easy

5 mins

1 hr

 **COOK'S TIP**

You can substitute other canned beans for the navy beans—try cannellini or garbanzo beans or black-eye peas instead. Rinse them before use because canned beans often have sugar or salt added.

The tomatoes in this recipe give the rice its distinctive pinkish color. The texture of the rice will be slightly "wet."

# Mexican Tomato Rice

**SERVES 6 – 8**

2 cups long-grain rice
1 large onion, chopped
2–3 garlic cloves, crushed
12 oz/350 g canned Italian plum tomatoes
3–4 tbsp olive oil
4 cups chicken bouillon
1 tbsp tomato paste
1 habañero or other hot chile
1½ cups frozen peas, thawed
4 tbsp chopped fresh cilantro
salt and pepper

*to serve*
1 large avocado, peeled, pitted, sliced, and sprinkled with lime juice
lime wedges
4 scallions, chopped
1 tbsp chopped fresh cilantro

**NUTRITION**
Calories *311*; Sugars *4 g*; Protein *7 g*;
Carbohydrate *50 g*; Fat *11 g*; Saturates *2 g*

easy

30 mins

40 mins

1 Cover the rice with hot water and set aside to stand for 15 minutes. Drain, then rinse under cold running water.

2 Place the onion and garlic in a food processor and process until a smooth purée forms. Scrape the purée into a small bowl and set aside. Put the tomatoes in the food processor and process until smooth, then strain into another bowl, pushing through any solids with the back of a wooden spoon.

3 Heat the oil in a flameproof casserole over medium heat. Add the rice and cook, stirring frequently, for 4 minutes until golden and translucent. Add the onion purée and cook, stirring frequently, for a further 2 minutes. Add the bouillon, processed canned tomatoes, and tomato paste and bring to a boil.

4 Using a pin or long needle, carefully pierce the chile in 2–3 places. Add to the rice, season to taste with salt and pepper, and reduce the heat to low. Cover and simmer for about 25 minutes until the rice is tender and the liquid just absorbed. Discard the chile, stir in the peas and cilantro, and cook for about 5 minutes to heat through.

5 To serve, gently fork the rice mixture into a warmed, large, shallow serving bowl. Arrange the avocado slices and lime wedges on top. Sprinkle over the chopped scallions and chopped cilantro and serve immediately.

A good quick supper for the family, this dish is incredibly simple to put together, yet is truly delicious.

# Baked Tomato Rice

1 Heat the vegetable oil in a large flameproof casserole over medium heat. Add the onion and red bell pepper and cook, stirring frequently, for about 5 minutes until soft and lightly colored. Stir in the garlic and thyme and cook for another minute.

2 Add the rice and cook, stirring frequently, for about 2 minutes until the rice is well coated and translucent. Stir in the bouillon, tomatoes, and bay leaf. Bring to a boil and simmer vigorously for 5 minutes until the bouillon is almost completely absorbed.

3 Stir in the basil, Cheddar cheese, chives, and pork sausages and bake, covered, in a preheated oven, 350°F/ 180°C, for about 25 minutes.

4 Sprinkle with the Parmesan cheese and return to the oven, uncovered, for 5 minutes until the top is golden.

**SERVES 4**

2 tbsp vegetable oil
1 onion, coarsely chopped
1 red bell pepper, seeded and chopped
2 garlic cloves, chopped finely
½ tsp dried thyme
1½ cups long-grain rice
4 cups chicken or vegetable bouillon
8 oz/225 g canned chopped tomatoes
1 bay leaf
2 tbsp shredded fresh basil
1½ cups grated sharp Cheddar cheese
2 tbsp chopped fresh chives
4 herbed pork sausages, cooked and cut into ½-inch/1-cm pieces
2–3 tbsp freshly grated Parmesan cheese

**NUTRITION**
Calories 708; Sugars 7 g; Protein 27 g; Carbohydrate 76 g; Fat 35 g; Saturates 16 g

  easy

  5 mins

  45 mins

🍳 **COOK'S TIP**

For a vegetarian version, replace the pork sausages with a 1½ cups canned, drained lima beans, kidney beans, or corn. Alternatively, try a mixture of sautéed mushrooms and zucchini.

This tasty risotto gets its vibrant green color from the spinach and mint. Serve with Italian-style rustic bread and salad for an informal supper.

# Minted Green Risotto

**SERVES 6**

2 tbsp sweet butter

4 cups fresh shelled peas or thawed frozen peas

2 lb 4 oz/1 kg young spinach leaves, washed and drained

1 bunch fresh mint, leaves stripped from stalks

2 tbsp chopped fresh basil

2 tbsp chopped fresh oregano

pinch of freshly grated nutmeg

4 tbsp mascarpone cheese or heavy cream

2 tbsp vegetable oil

1 onion, chopped finely

4 celery stalks, including leaves, chopped finely

2 garlic cloves, chopped finely

½ tsp dried thyme

2⅔ cups risotto rice

¼ cup dry white vermouth

4 cups chicken or vegetable bouillon, simmering

1 cup freshly grated Parmesan cheese

**NUTRITION**

Calories 512; Sugars 7 g; Protein 20 g; Carbohydrate 51 g; Fat 24 g; Saturates 12 g

  easy

10 mins

35 mins

1 Heat half the butter in a deep skillet over medium-high heat until sizzling. Add the peas, spinach, mint leaves, basil, and oregano and season with the nutmeg. Cook, stirring frequently, for about 3 minutes until the spinach and mint leaves are wilted. Cool slightly.

2 Pour the spinach mixture into a food processor and process for 15 seconds. Add the mascarpone or cream and process again for about 1 minute. Transfer to a bowl and set aside.

3 Heat the oil and remaining butter in a large, heavy pan over medium heat. Add the onion, celery, garlic, and thyme and cook for about 2 minutes until the vegetables are softened. Add the rice and cook, stirring frequently, for about 2 minutes until the rice is translucent and well coated.

4 Add the vermouth to the rice; it will bubble and steam rapidly. When it is almost absorbed, add a ladleful (about 1 cup) of the simmering bouillon. Cook, stirring constantly, until the bouillon is completely absorbed.

5 Continue adding the bouillon, about half a cup at a time, allowing each addition to be absorbed before adding the next. This should take 20–25 minutes. The risotto should have a creamy consistency and the rice should be just tender. Stir in the spinach-cream mixture and the Parmesan. Serve the risotto immediately.

The beets and red wine give this risotto its stunning color and also impart a rich sweet flavor, which is unusual but surprisingly delicious.

# Hot Pink Risotto

1 Put the dried cherries or cranberries in a pan with the wine and bring to a boil. Simmer for 2–3 minutes until slightly reduced. Remove from the heat and set aside.

2 Heat the oil in a large heavy pan over medium heat. Add the onion, celery, and thyme and cook, stirring occasionally, for about 2 minutes until just beginning to soften. Add the garlic and rice and cook, stirring constantly, until the rice is well coated.

3 Add a ladleful (about 1 cup) of the simmering bouillon; it will bubble and steam rapidly. Cook, stirring constantly, until the liquid is absorbed.

4 Continue adding the bouillon, about half a cup at a time, allowing each addition to be absorbed before adding the next. This should take 20–25 minutes. The risotto should have a creamy consistency and the rice should be tender, but firm to the bite. Halfway through the cooking time, remove the cherries or cranberries from the wine with a draining spoon and add to the risotto with the beets and half the wine. Continue adding the bouillon or remaining wine.

5 Stir in the dill and chives and season to taste with salt and pepper. Serve with the Parmesan, if wished.

SERVES   4 – 6

1½ cups dried sour cherries or dried cranberries
1 cup fruity red wine, such as Valpolicella
3 tbsp olive oil
1 large red onion, chopped finely
2 celery stalks, chopped finely
½ tsp dried thyme
1 garlic clove, chopped finely
3 cups risotto rice
5 cups chicken or vegetable bouillon, simmering
4 cooked beet (not in vinegar), diced
2 tbsp chopped fresh dill
2 tbsp chopped fresh chives
salt and pepper
⅔ cup freshly grated Parmesan cheese, to serve (optional)

**NUTRITION**
Calories 397; Sugars 9 g; Protein 11 g; Carbohydrate 61 g; Fat 11 g; Saturates 3 g

 easy

10 mins

40 mins

Although this is the easiest, most basic risotto, it is one of the most delicious. Because there are few ingredients, use the best of each.

# Easy Cheese Risotto

**SERVES 4–6**

4–6 tbsp sweet butter
1 onion, chopped finely
2²⁄₃ cups risotto rice
½ cup dry white vermouth or white wine
5 cups chicken or vegetable bouillon, simmering
1 cup freshly grated Parmesan cheese, plus extra for sprinkling
salt and pepper

1 Heat about 2 tablespoons of the butter in a large heavy pan over medium heat. Add the onion and cook for about 2 minutes until just beginning to soften. Add the rice and cook, stirring frequently, for about 2 minutes until translucent and well coated with the butter.

2 Pour in the vermouth: it will bubble and steam rapidly and evaporate almost immediately. Add a ladleful (about 1 cup) of the simmering bouillon and cook, stirring constantly, until the liquid is completely absorbed.

3 Continue adding the bouillon, about half a cup at a time, allowing each addition to be absorbed before adding the next—never allow the rice to cook "dry." This should take 20–25 minutes. The risotto should have a creamy consistency and the rice grains should be tender, but still firm to the bite.

4 Switch off the heat and stir in the remaining butter and the grated Parmesan cheese. Season with salt and pepper to taste. Cover the pan, let stand for about 1 minute, then serve with extra Parmesan for sprinkling.

**NUTRITION**
Calories 353; Sugars 2 g; Protein 10 g;
Carbohydrate 40 g; Fat 15 g; Saturates 9 g

easy

5 mins

30 mins

 **COOK'S TIP**

If you prefer not to use butter, soften the onion in 2 tablespoons olive oil and stir in about 2 tablespoons extra virgin olive oil with the Parmesan at the end.

It's worth searching around for wild arugula because its robust, peppery flavor makes all the difference to this dish.

# Tomato *and* Arugula Risotto

1 Heat the oil and half the butter in a large skillet. Add the onion and cook for about 2 minutes until just beginning to soften. Stir in the garlic and rice and cook, stirring frequently, until the rice is translucent and well coated.

2 Pour in the vermouth; it will evaporate almost immediately. Add a ladleful (about 1 cup) of the bouillon and cook, stirring, until it is absorbed.

3 Continue adding the bouillon, about half a cup at a time, allowing each addition to be absorbed before adding the next. Just before the rice is tender, stir in the chopped tomatoes and arugula. Shred the basil leaves and immediately stir into the risotto. Continue to cook, adding more bouillon, until the risotto is creamy and the rice is tender, but firm to the bite.

4 Remove from the heat and stir in the remaining butter, the grated Parmesan, and mozzarella. Season to taste with salt and pepper. Remove the pan from the heat, cover, and let stand for about 1 minute. Serve immediately, before the mozzarella melts completely.

## SERVES 4–6

2 tbsp olive oil
2 tbsp sweet butter
1 large onion, chopped finely
2 garlic cloves, chopped finely
3 cups risotto rice
½ cup dry white vermouth
6 cups chicken or vegetable bouillon, simmering
6 vine-ripened or Italian plum tomatoes, seeded and chopped
4 oz/126 g wild arugula
handful of fresh basil leaves
1⅓ cups freshly grated Parmesan cheese
2 cups coarsely grated or diced fresh Italian buffalo mozzarella
salt and pepper

## NUTRITION
Calories 546; Sugars 6 g; Protein 23 g; Carbohydrate 57 g; Fat 24 g; Saturates 12 g

 easy

 10 mins

 30 mins

Make this creamy risotto with Italian arborio rice and freshly grated Parmesan cheese for the best results.

# Mushroom *and* Cheese Risotto

**SERVES 4**

2 tbsp olive or vegetable oil
2 cups risotto rice
2 garlic cloves, crushed
1 onion, chopped
2 celery stalks, chopped
1 red or green bell pepper, seeded and
   chopped
3¼ cups sliced mushrooms
1 tbsp chopped fresh oregano or 1 tsp dried
   oregano
4 cups vegetable bouillon
½ cup sun-dried tomatoes in olive oil,
   drained and chopped (optional)
⅔ cup finely grated Parmesan cheese
salt and pepper

*to garnish*
sprigs of fresh flatleaf parsley
fresh bay leaves

1 Heat the oil in a wok or large skillet. Add the rice and cook, stirring constantly, for 5 minutes.

2 Add the garlic, onion, celery, and bell pepper and cook, stirring constantly, for 5 minutes. Add the mushrooms and cook for 3–4 minutes.

3 Stir in the oregano and bouillon. Heat until just boiling, then reduce the heat, cover, and simmer gently for about 20 minutes or until the rice is tender and creamy.

4 Add the sun-dried tomatoes, if using, and season to taste with salt and pepper. Stir in half of the grated Parmesan cheese. Top with the remaining cheese, garnish with flatleaf parsley and bay leaves, and serve.

**NUTRITION**
Calories *358*; Sugars *3 g*; Protein *11 g*;
Carbohydrate *50 g*; Fat *14 g*; Saturates *5 g*

easy

20 mins

40 mins

This fragrant risotto makes a delicate first course for a special meal. Serve with grated Parmesan, if desired.

# Orange-Scented Risotto

1 Toast the pine nuts in a skillet over medium heat for about 3 minutes, stirring and shaking frequently, until golden brown. Set aside.

2 Heat half the butter in a large, heavy pan over medium heat. Add the shallots and leek and cook for about 2 minutes until they begin to soften. Add the rice and cook, stirring frequently, for about 2 minutes until the rice is translucent and well coated.

3 Pour in the liqueur or vermouth; it will evaporate almost immediately. Add a ladleful (about 1 cup) of the bouillon and cook, stirring, until absorbed. Continue adding the bouillon, about half a cup at a time, allowing each addition to be absorbed before adding the next—never allow the rice to cook "dry."

4 After about 15 minutes, add the orange rind and juice and continue to cook, adding more bouillon, until the rice is tender, but firm to the bite, and all the liquid has been absorbed. The risotto should have a creamy consistency.

5 Remove from the heat and stir in the remaining butter and 2 tablespoons of the chives. Season to taste with salt and pepper. Spoon into serving dishes and sprinkle with the toasted pine nuts and the remaining chives.

**SERVES 4**

2 tbsp pine nuts
4 tbsp sweet butter
2 shallots, chopped finely
1 leek, shredded finely
3½ cups risotto rice
2 tbsp orange-flavored liqueur or dry white vermouth
6¼ cups chicken or vegetable bouillon, simmering
grated rind of 1 orange
juice of 2 oranges, strained
3 tbsp chopped fresh chives
salt and pepper

**NUTRITION**
Calories 599; Sugars 9 g; Protein 10 g; Carbohydrate 95 g; Fat 22 g; Saturates 9 g

✪✪✪     moderate

    10 mins

     35 mins

Paella traditionally
contains chicken and fish,
but this recipe is packed
with vegetables and nuts
for a truly delicious and
simple vegetarian dish.

# Cashew Nut Paella

**SERVES 4**

2 tbsp olive oil
1 tbsp butter
1 red onion, chopped
2/3 cup risotto rice
1 tsp ground turmeric
1 tsp ground cumin
1/2 tsp chili powder
3 garlic cloves, crushed
1 fresh green chile, seeded and sliced
1 green bell pepper, seeded and diced
1 red bell pepper, seeded and diced
3/4 cup baby corn cobs, halved lengthwise
2 tbsp pitted black olives
1 large tomato, seeded and diced
2 cups vegetable bouillon
3/4 cup unsalted cashew nuts
1/2 cup frozen peas
2 tbsp chopped fresh parsley
pinch of cayenne pepper
salt and pepper
fresh herbs, to garnish

**NUTRITION**
Calories 406; Sugars 8 g; Protein 10 g;
Carbohydrate 44 g; Fat 22 g; Saturates 6 g

easy

15 mins

35 mins

1 Heat the olive oil and butter in a large skillet or paella pan until the butter has melted.

2 Add the onion and cook over medium heat, stirring constantly, for about 2–3 minutes until softened.

3 Stir in the rice, turmeric, cumin, chili powder, garlic, sliced chile, green and red bell peppers, corn cobs, olives, and tomato and cook over medium heat, stirring occasionally, for 1–2 minutes.

4 Pour in the bouillon and bring the mixture to a boil. Reduce the heat and cook gently, stirring constantly, for 20 minutes.

5 Add the cashew nuts and peas and cook, stirring occasionally, for a further 5 minutes. Season to taste with salt and pepper and sprinkle with parsley and cayenne pepper. Transfer to warm serving plates, garnish with fresh herbs, and serve immediately.

This is a hearty and flavorful soup that is good on its own or spooned over cooked rice or baked potatoes for a more substantial meal.

# Vegetable Chili

1 Brush the eggplant slices on 1 side with olive oil. Heat half the oil in a large, heavy skillet over medium-high heat. Add the eggplant slices, oiled-side up, and cook for 5–6 minutes until browned on 1 side. Turn the slices over, cook on the other side until browned and then transfer to a plate. Cut the slices into bite-size pieces.

2 Heat the remaining oil in a large pan over medium heat. Add the onion and bell peppers and cook, stirring occasionally, for 3–4 minutes until the onion is just softened, but not browned. Add the garlic and continue cooking for 2–3 minutes or until the onion is just beginning to color.

3 Add the tomatoes, chili powder, cumin, and oregano. Season to taste with salt and pepper. Bring just to a boil, reduce the heat, cover, and simmer gently for 15 minutes.

4 Add the zucchini, eggplant pieces, and kidney beans. Stir in the water and tomato paste. Bring back to a boil, cover, and continue simmering for about 45 minutes or until the vegetables are tender. Adjust the seasoning if necessary. If you prefer a hotter dish, stir in a little more chili powder.

5 Ladle into warmed bowls and top with scallions and cheese.

SERVES 4

1 medium eggplant, peeled if wished, cut into 1-inch/2.5-cm slices
1 tbsp olive oil, plus extra for brushing
1 large red or yellow onion, chopped finely
2 red or yellow bell peppers, seeded and chopped finely
3–4 garlic cloves, chopped finely or crushed
1 lb 12 oz/800g canned chopped tomatoes
1 tbsp mild chili powder
½ tsp ground cumin
½ tsp dried oregano
2 small zucchini, quartered lengthwise and sliced
14 oz/400g canned kidney beans, drained and rinsed
2 cups water
1 tbsp tomato paste
6 scallions, chopped finely
1 cup grated Cheddar cheese
salt and pepper

NUTRITION
Calories 213; Sugars 11 g; Protein 12 g; Carbohydrate 21 g; Fat 10 g; Saturates 5 g

⊛⊛     easy
        10 mins
        1 hr 15 mins

Millet makes an interesting alternative to rice, which is the more traditional ingredient for a pilau. Serve with a crisp Asian salad.

# Asian-Style Millet Pilau

**SERVES 4**

1½ cups millet grains
1 tbsp vegetable oil
1 bunch scallions, white and green parts, chopped
1 garlic clove, crushed
1 tsp grated fresh gingerroot
1 orange bell pepper, seeded and diced
2½ cups water
1 orange
⅔ cup chopped pitted dates
2 tsp sesame oil
1 cup roasted cashew nuts
2 tbsp pumpkin seeds
salt and pepper
Asian salad vegetables, to serve

1 Place the millet in a large pan and toast over medium heat, shaking the pan occasionally, for 4–5 minutes until the grains begin to crack and pop.

2 Heat the oil in another pan. Add the scallions, garlic, gingerroot, and bell pepper and cook over medium heat, stirring frequently, for 2–3 minutes until just softened, but not browned. Add the millet and pour in the water.

3 Using a vegetable peeler, pare the rind from the orange and add the rind to the pan. Squeeze the juice from the orange into the pan. Season to taste with salt and pepper.

4 Bring to a boil, reduce the heat, cover, and cook gently for 20 minutes until all the liquid has been absorbed. Remove the pan from the heat, stir in the dates and sesame oil, and set aside to stand for 10 minutes.

5 Remove and discard the orange rind and stir in the cashew nuts. Pile into a warmed serving dish, sprinkle with pumpkin seeds, and serve immediately with Asian salad vegetables.

**NUTRITION**
Calories *660*; Sugars *28 g*; Protein *15 g*;
Carbohydrate *94 g*; Fat *27 g*; Saturates *5 g*

easy

20 mins

30 mins

This colorful and interesting mixture of vegetables, cooked in a spicy sauce, is excellent served with rice and nan bread.

# Vegetable Curry

1 Cut the turnips or rutabaga, eggplant, and potatoes into ½-inch/1-cm cubes. Leave the mushrooms whole or slice them thickly if preferred. Slice the onion and carrots.

2 Heat the ghee or oil in a large pan. Add the onion, turnip or rutabaga, potato, and cauliflower and cook over low heat, stirring frequently, for 3 minutes.

3 Add the garlic, gingerroot, chiles, paprika, ground coriander, and curry powder or paste and cook, stirring, for 1 minute.

4 Add the bouillon, tomatoes, eggplant, and mushrooms and season with salt. Cover and simmer, stirring occasionally, for about 30 minutes or until tender. Add the green bell pepper and carrots, cover, and cook for another 5 minutes.

5 Blend the cornstarch with the coconut milk to a smooth paste and stir into the mixture. Add the ground almonds and simmer, stirring constantly, for 2 minutes. Taste and adjust the seasoning if necessary. Transfer the curry to serving plates and serve hot, garnished with sprigs of fresh cilantro.

SERVES 4

8 oz/225 g turnips or rutabaga
1 eggplant
12 oz/350 g new potatoes
2 cups cauliflower florets
8 oz/225 g white mushrooms
1 large onion
3 carrots
6 tbsp vegetable ghee or vegetable oil
2 garlic cloves, crushed
4 tsp finely chopped fresh gingerroot
1–2 fresh green chiles, seeded and chopped
1 tbsp paprika
2 tsp ground coriander
1 tbsp mild or medium curry powder or paste
2 cups vegetable bouillon
14 oz/400g canned chopped tomatoes
1 green bell pepper, seeded and sliced
1 tbsp cornstarch
⅔ cup coconut milk
2–3 tbsp ground almonds
salt
sprigs of fresh cilantro, to garnish

**NUTRITION**
Calories *421*; Sugars *20 g*; Protein *12 g*; Carbohydrate *42 g*; Fat *24 g*; Saturates *3 g*

easy

10 mins

45 mins

This unusual vegetarian dish is best served as a side dish with other curries and with rice to soak up the wonderfully rich, spiced juices.

# Spiced Cashew Nut Curry

### SERVES 4

2¼ cups unsalted cashew nuts
1 tsp coriander seeds
1 tsp cumin seeds
2 cardamom pods, crushed
1 tbsp sunflower oil
1 onion, sliced thinly
1 garlic clove, crushed
1 small fresh green chile, seeded and
    chopped
1 cinnamon stick
½ tsp ground turmeric
4 tbsp coconut cream
1¼ cups hot vegetable bouillon
3 kaffir lime leaves, shredded finely
salt and pepper
boiled jasmine rice, to serve

1 Soak the cashew nuts in cold water overnight. Drain thoroughly. Crush the coriander seeds, cumin seeds, and cardamom pods with a mortar and pestle.

2 Heat the oil and stir-fry the onion and garlic for 2–3 minutes to soften, but not brown. Add the chile, crushed spices, cinnamon stick, and turmeric and stir-fry for a further minute.

3 Add the coconut cream and the hot bouillon to the pan. Bring to a boil, then add the cashew nuts and lime leaves.

4 Cover the pan, lower the heat, and simmer for about 20 minutes. Serve hot, accompanied by jasmine rice.

### NUTRITION
Calories 455; Sugars 6 g; Protein 13 g;
Carbohydrate 16 g; Fat 39 g; Saturates 11 g

 very easy

8 hrs 15 mins

 25 mins

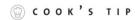 COOK'S TIP

All spices give the best flavor when freshly crushed, but if you prefer, you can use ground spices instead of crushing them yourself in a mortar with a pestle.

This is a wonderfully quick dish to prepare. If you don't have time to prepare the curry paste, it can be bought ready-made.

# Red Curry *with* Cashews

1 To make the curry paste, grind all the ingredients in a large mortar with a pestle or in a grinder. Alternatively, process briefly in a food processor. (The quantity of red curry paste is more than is required for this recipe. Store for up to 3 weeks in a sealed jar in the refrigerator.)

2 Put a wok or, heavy-based skillet over high heat, add 3 tablespoons of the red curry paste, and stir until it gives off its aroma. Reduce the heat to medium.

3 Add the coconut milk, kaffir lime leaf, light soy sauce, baby corn cobs, broccoli florets, green beans, and cashew nuts. Bring to a boil and simmer for about 10 minutes until the vegetables are cooked, but still firm and crunchy.

4 Remove and discard the lime leaf and stir in the basil leaves and cilantro. Transfer to a warmed serving dish, garnish with peanuts, and serve.

**SERVES  4**

generous 1 cup coconut milk
1 kaffir lime leaf
¼ tsp light soy sauce
4 baby corn cobs, halved lengthwise
1 cup broccoli florets
4½ oz/115 g green beans, cut into
    2-inch/5-cm pieces
4 tbsp cashew nuts
15 fresh basil leaves
1 tbsp chopped fresh cilantro
1 tbsp chopped roasted peanuts, to garnish

*red curry paste*

7 fresh red chiles, seeded and blanched
2 tsp cumin seeds
2 tsp coriander seeds
1-inch/2.5-cm piece of galangal, chopped
½ lemongrass stalk, chopped
1 tsp salt
grated rind of 1 lime
4 garlic cloves, chopped
3 shallots, chopped
2 kaffir lime leaves, shredded
1 tbsp vegetable oil

**NUTRITION**
Calories *274*; Sugars *5 g*; Protein *10 g*;
Carbohydrate *38 g*; Fat *10 g*; Saturates *3 g*

⭐⭐      easy

      25 mins

      15 mins

A mildly spiced but richly flavored Indian-style dish full of different textures and flavors. Serve with nan bread to soak up the tasty sauce.

# Coconut Vegetable Curry

**SERVES 4**

1 large eggplant, cut into 1-inch/ 2.5-cm cubes
2 tbsp vegetable oil
2 garlic cloves, crushed
1 fresh green chile, seeded and chopped finely
1 tsp grated fresh gingerroot
1 onion, chopped finely
2 tsp garam masala
8 cardamom pods
1 tsp ground turmeric
1 tbsp tomato paste
3 cups Fresh Vegetable Bouillon (see page 14)
1 tbsp lemon juice
8 oz/225 g potatoes, diced
2 cups small cauliflower florets
8 oz/225 g okra, trimmed
2 cups frozen peas
²⁄₃ cup coconut milk
salt and pepper
flaked coconut, to garnish
nan bread, to serve

**NUTRITION**
Calories *159*; Sugars *8 g*; Protein *8 g*;
Carbohydrate *19 g*; Fat *6 g*; Saturates *1 g*

easy

1 hr 45 mins

35 mins

1 Layer the eggplant in a bowl, sprinkling with salt as you go. Set aside for 30 minutes. Rinse well under cold running water. Drain and dry. Set aside.

2 Heat the oil in a large pan and gently cook the garlic, chile, gingerroot, onion, and spices for 4–5 minutes.

3 Stir in the tomato paste, bouillon, lemon juice, potatoes, and cauliflower and mix well. Bring to a boil, cover, and simmer for 15 minutes.

4 Stir in the eggplant, okra, peas, and coconut milk and season with salt and pepper to taste. Continue to simmer, uncovered, for a further 10 minutes until tender. Discard the cardamom pods. Pile the curry on to a warmed serving platter, garnish with flaked coconut, and serve with nan bread.

Potatoes are not highly regarded in Thai cooking because rice is the traditional staple. This dish is a tasty exception.

# Yellow Curry

1 Place the garlic, galangal, lemongrass, and coriander seeds in a mortar and pound continuously with a pestle until a smooth paste forms.

2 Heat 2 tablespoons of the oil in a skillet or wok. Stir in the garlic paste and stir-fry for 30 seconds. Stir in the curry paste and turmeric, then add the coconut milk, and bring the mixture to a boil.

3 Add the potatoes and bouillon. Return to a boil, then lower the heat, and simmer, uncovered, for 10–12 minutes, until the potatoes are almost tender.

4 Stir in the spinach and simmer until the leaves are wilted.

5 Cook the onion in the remaining oil until crisp and golden brown. Place on top of the curry just before serving.

**SERVES 4**

2 garlic cloves, chopped finely
1¼-inch/3-cm piece of galangal, chopped finely
1 lemongrass stalk, chopped finely
1 tsp coriander seeds
3 tbsp vegetable oil
2 tsp Thai red curry paste
½ tsp ground turmeric
scant 1 cup coconut milk
2 cups cubed potatoes
scant ½ cup vegetable bouillon
3 tightly packed cups young spinach leaves
1 small onion, sliced thinly into rings

**NUTRITION**
Calories 160; Sugars 4 g; Protein 3 g; Carbohydrate 15 g; Fat 10 g; Saturates 1 g

  easy

5 mins

15 mins

 **COOK'S TIP**

Choose a firm potato for this dish, one that will keep its shape during cooking, in preference to a mealy variety that will break up easily once cooked.

Seasonal fresh vegetables are casseroled with lentils, then topped with a ring of fresh cheese biscuits to make this tasty cobbler.

# Winter Vegetable Pot Pie

**SERVES 4**

1 tbsp olive oil
1 garlic clove, crushed
8 small onions, halved
2 celery stalks, sliced
2 cups chopped rutabaga
2 carrots, sliced
½ small cauliflower, broken into florets
3¼ cups sliced mushrooms
14 oz/400 g canned chopped tomatoes
¼ cup red lentils, washed
2 tbsp cornstarch
3–4 tbsp water
1¼ cups vegetable bouillon
2 tsp Tabasco sauce
2 tsp chopped fresh oregano
sprigs of fresh oregano, to garnish

*pot pie topping*
2 cups self-rising flour
4 tbsp butter
1 cup grated sharp Cheddar cheese
2 tsp chopped fresh oregano
1 egg, lightly beaten
⅔ cup milk
salt

**NUTRITION**

Calories *734*; Sugars *22 g*; Protein *27 g*;
Carbohydrate *96 g*; Fat *30 g*; Saturates *16 g*

moderate

20 mins

40 mins

1 Heat the oil and cook the garlic and onions for 5 minutes. Add the celery, rutabaga, carrots, and cauliflower and cook for 2–3 minutes. Add the mushrooms, tomatoes, and lentils. Mix the cornstarch and water and stir into the pan with the bouillon, Tabasco, and oregano.

2 Transfer to an ovenproof dish, cover, and bake in a preheated oven, 350°F/ 180°C, for 20 minutes.

3 To make the topping, sift the flour with a pinch of salt into a bowl. Rub in the butter, then stir in most of the cheese and the chopped herbs. Beat the egg with the milk and add enough to the dry ingredients to make a soft dough. Knead, roll out to ½ inch/1 cm thick and cut into 2-inch/5-cm rounds.

4 Remove the dish from the oven and increase the temperature to 400°F/200°C. Arrange the biscuits around the edge of the casserole, brush with the remaining egg and milk, and sprinkle with the reserved cheese. Cook for another 10–12 minutes. Garnish and serve.

This is a really hearty dish, perfect for winter days when a filling hot dish is just what you need to keep the cold out.

# Lentil *and* Rice Casserole

1 Place the lentils, rice, and vegetable bouillon in a large flameproof casserole and cook over low heat, stirring occasionally, for 20 minutes.

2 Add the leek, garlic, tomatoes and their can juice, ground cumin, chili powder, garam masala, sliced bell pepper, broccoli, corn cobs, and green beans to the casserole.

3 Bring the mixture to a boil, reduce the heat, cover, and simmer for another 10–15 minutes or until all the vegetables are tender.

4 Add the shredded basil and season with salt and pepper to taste.

5 Garnish with fresh basil sprigs and serve immediately.

## SERVES 4

1 cup split red lentils, washed
generous ¼ cup long-grain rice
5 cups vegetable bouillon
1 leek, cut into chunks
3 garlic cloves, crushed
14 oz/400 g canned chopped tomatoes
1 tsp ground cumin
1 tsp chili powder
1 tsp garam masala
1 red bell pepper, seeded and sliced
1 cup small broccoli flowerets
8 baby corn cobs, halved lengthwise
½ cup green beans, halved
1 tbsp shredded fresh basil
salt and pepper
sprigs of fresh basil, to garnish

## NUTRITION

Calories 312; Sugars 9 g; Protein 20 g; Carbohydrate 51 g; Fat 2 g; Saturates 0.4 g

 ⭐⭐ easy

🕐 15 mins

🕐 20 mins

 **COOK'S TIP**

You can vary the rice in this recipe—use brown or wild rice, if you prefer.

The tomatoes are a great contrast to the cauliflower and herbs, making this dish appealing to both the eye and the palate.

# Cauliflower Bake

**SERVES 4**

4 cups cauliflower, broken into florets
4½ cups cubed potatoes
8 cherry tomatoes

*sauce*

2 tbsp butter or margarine
1 leek, sliced
1 garlic clove, crushed
3 tbsp all-purpose flour
1¼ cups milk
¾ cup grated mixed cheese, such as
　Cheddar, Parmesan, and Swiss
½ tsp paprika
2 tbsp chopped fresh flatleaf parsley
salt and pepper
chopped fresh parsley, to garnish

1 Cook the cauliflower in a pan of boiling water for 10 minutes. Drain well and reserve. Meanwhile, cook the potatoes in another pan of boiling water for 10 minutes, drain, and reserve.

2 To make the sauce, melt the butter or margarine in a pan and sauté the leek and garlic for 1 minute. Stir in the flour and cook, stirring constantly, for 1 minute. Remove the pan from the heat and gradually stir in the milk, ½ cup of the grated cheese, the paprika, and flatleaf parsley. Return the pan to the heat and bring to a boil, stirring constantly. Season with salt and pepper.

3 Spoon the cauliflower into a deep casserole. Add the cherry tomatoes and top with the potatoes. Pour the sauce over the potatoes and sprinkle on the remaining cheese.

4 Cook in a preheated oven, 350°F/180°C, for 20 minutes or until the vegetables are cooked through and the cheese is golden-brown and bubbling. Garnish and serve immediately.

**NUTRITION**
Calories *305*; Sugars *9 g*; Protein *15 g*;
Carbohydrate *31 g*; Fat *14 g*; Saturates *6 g*

easy

10 mins

40 mins

 **COOK'S TIP**

This dish could be made with broccoli instead of cauliflower.

This is a very colorful and nutritious dish, packed full of crunchy vegetables in a tasty white wine sauce.

# Potato-Topped Vegetables

1 Cook the carrot, cauliflower, broccoli, fennel, and beans in a large pan of boiling water for 10 minutes until just tender. Drain the vegetables thoroughly and set aside.

2 Melt the butter in a pan. Stir in the flour and cook for 1 minute. Remove from the heat and stir in the bouillon, wine, and milk. Return to the heat and bring to a boil, stirring until thickened. Stir in the reserved vegetables, mushrooms, and sage.

3 Meanwhile, make the topping. Cook the potatoes in boiling water for 10–15 minutes. Drain thoroughly and mash with the butter, yogurt, and half the grated cheese. Stir in the fennel seeds. Season to taste.

4 Spoon the vegetable mixture into a 4-cup pie dish. Spoon the mashed potato over the top and sprinkle with the remaining cheese. Cook in a preheated oven, 375°F/190°C, for 30–35 minutes or until golden. Serve hot.

**SERVES 4**

1 carrot, diced
1½ cups cauliflower florets
1½ cups broccoli florets
1 fennel bulb, sliced
¾ cup green beans, halved
2 tbsp butter
2½ tbsp all-purpose flour
⅔ cup vegetable bouillon
⅔ cup dry white wine
⅔ cup milk
6 oz/175 g crimini mushrooms, quartered
2 tbsp chopped fresh sage

*topping*
2 lb/900 g mealy potatoes, diced
2 tbsp butter
4 tbsp plain yogurt
scant 1 cup freshly grated Parmesan cheese
1 tsp fennel seeds
salt and pepper

**NUTRITION**
Calories *413* Sugars *11 g*; Protein *19 g*;
Carbohydrate *41 g*; Fat *18 g*; Saturates *11 g*

 easy

20 mins

 1 hr 15 mins

This satisfying dish can be cooked in a single large dish or in four individual muffin pans.

# Vegetable Toad -in-the-Hole

**SERVES 4**

*batter*
¾ cup all-purpose flour
2 eggs, beaten
¾ cup milk
2 tbsp whole-grain mustard
2 tbsp vegetable oil

*filling*
2 tbsp butter
2 garlic cloves, crushed
1 onion, cut into eight
18 baby carrots, halved lengthwise
⅔ cup green beans
¼ cup canned corn, drained
2 tomatoes, seeded and cut into chunks
1 tsp whole-grain mustard
1 tbsp chopped mixed herbs
salt and pepper

1 To make the batter, strain the flour and a pinch of salt into a bowl. Beat in the eggs and milk to make a batter. Stir in the mustard and let stand.

2 Pour the oil into a shallow ovenproof dish and heat in a preheated oven, 400°F/200°C, for 10 minutes.

3 To make the filling, melt the butter in a skillet and sauté the garlic and onion, stirring constantly, for 2 minutes. Cook the carrots and beans in a pan of boiling water for 7 minutes, or until tender. Drain well.

4 Add the corn and tomatoes to the skillet with the mustard and chopped mixed herbs. Season well and add the carrots and beans.

5 Remove the heated dish from the oven and pour in the batter. Spoon the vegetables into the center, return to the oven, and cook for 30–35 minutes, until the batter has risen and set. Serve immediately.

**NUTRITION**
Calories 313; Sugars 9 g; Protein 9 g;
Carbohydrate 31 g; Fat 18 g; Saturates 7 g

moderate

15 mins

55 mins

This is a dish of Persian origin, not Chinese as it sounds. Eggplants are fried and mixed with tomatoes, mint, sugar, and vinegar.

# Sweet *and* Sour Vegetables

1 Using a sharp knife, cut the eggplants into cubes. Put them in a colander, sprinkle with plenty of salt, and let stand for 30 minutes. Rinse well under cold running water to remove all traces of the salt and drain thoroughly. This process removes all the bitter juices from the eggplants. Pat dry with paper towels.

2 Heat the oil in a large, heavy-based skillet.

3 Add the eggplants and sauté over medium heat, stirring, for 1–2 minutes, until beginning to color.

4 Stir in the garlic and onion wedges and cook, stirring constantly, for another 2–3 minutes.

5 Stir in the tomatoes, mint, and vegetable bouillon. Lower the heat, cover with a lid, and simmer for about 15–20 minutes, or until the eggplant is tender.

6 Add the brown sugar, red wine vinegar, and chile flakes, then season with salt and pepper according to taste and cook for another 2–3 minutes, stirring constantly.

7 Transfer to a warmed serving dish, garnish the eggplant with fresh mint sprigs and serve immediately.

SERVES  4

2 large eggplants
6 tbsp olive oil
4 garlic cloves, crushed
1 onion, cut into eight
4 large tomatoes, seeded and chopped
3 tbsp chopped mint
²/₃ cup vegetable bouillon
4 tsp brown sugar
2 tbsp red wine vinegar
1 tsp chile flakes
salt and pepper
sprigs of fresh mint, to garnish

NUTRITION
Calories *218*; Sugars *12 g*; Protein *3 g*;
Carbohydrate *14 g*; Fat *17 g*; Saturates *3 g*

⭐⭐         easy

            45 mins

            30 mins

This colorful and tasty lasagna has layers of sliced eggplants and vegetables in tomato sauce, all topped with a rich cheese sauce.

# Vegetable Lasagna

**SERVES 4**

1 eggplant, sliced
3 tbsp olive oil
2 garlic cloves, crushed
1 red onion, halved and sliced
3 mixed bell peppers, seeded and diced
½ lb/225 g mixed mushrooms, sliced
2 celery stalks, sliced
1 zucchini, diced
½ tsp chili powder
½ tsp ground cumin
2 tomatoes, chopped
1¼ cups crushed tomatoes
2 tbsp chopped basil
8 no-precook lasagna verde sheets
salt and pepper

*cheese sauce*

2 tbsp butter or margarine
1 tbsp flour
⅔ cup vegetable bouillon
1¼ cups milk
¾ cup grated Cheddar cheese
1 tsp Dijon mustard
1 tbsp chopped basil
1 egg, beaten

**NUTRITION**

Calories *544*; Sugars *18 g*; Protein *20 g*;
Carbohydrate *61 g*; Fat *26 g*; Saturates *12 g*

   easy

🕐   35 mins

🕐   55 mins

1 Place the eggplant slices in a colander, sprinkle them with salt, and let stand for 20 minutes. Rinse under cold running water, drain, and reserve.

2 Heat the oil in a pan and sauté the garlic and onion for 1–2 minutes. Add the bell peppers, mushrooms, celery, and zucchini and cook, stirring constantly, for 3–4 minutes.

3 Stir in the spices and cook for 1 minute. Mix in the chopped tomatoes, crushed tomatoes, and basil and season to taste with salt and pepper.

4 For the sauce, melt the butter in a pan, stir in the flour, and cook for 1 minute. Remove from the heat, stir in the bouillon and milk, return to the heat, and add half the cheese and all the mustard. Boil, stirring, until thickened. Stir in the basil. Remove from the heat and stir in the egg.

5 Place half the lasagna sheets in an ovenproof dish. Top with half the vegetable mixture then half the eggplants. Repeat the layers and spoon the cheese sauce over the top.

6 Sprinkle the lasagna with the remaining cheese and cook in a preheated oven, 350°F/180°C, for 40 minutes, until the top is golden-brown.

This is a really simple, family dish which is inexpensive and easy to prepare and cook. Serve with a salad or fresh green vegetables.

# Macaroni Cheese *and* Tomato

1 To make the tomato sauce, heat the oil in a heavy pan. Add the shallots and garlic and cook, stirring constantly, for 1 minute. Add the tomatoes and basil and season with salt and pepper to taste. Cook over medium heat, stirring constantly, for 10 minutes.

2 Meanwhile, bring a large pan of lightly salted water to a boil. Add the macaroni, bring back to a boil, and cook for 8 minutes or until tender, but still firm to the bite. Drain well.

3 Combine the grated Cheddar and Parmesan in a bowl. Grease a deep casserole. Spoon one third of the tomato sauce into the bottom of the dish, cover with one third of the macaroni, and then top with one third of the mixed cheeses. Season to taste with salt and pepper. Repeat these layers twice, ending with a layer of grated cheese.

4 Combine the bread crumbs and basil and sprinkle evenly over the top. Dot the topping with the butter or margarine and cook in a preheated oven, 375°F/190°C, for 25 minutes or until the the topping is golden-brown and bubbling. Serve immediately.

**SERVES 4**

2 cups dried elbow macaroni
1½ cups grated Cheddar cheese
generous 1 cup grated Parmesan cheese
1 tbsp butter or margarine, plus extra for greasing
4 tbsp fresh white bread crumbs
1 tbsp chopped fresh basil

*tomato sauce*
1 tbsp olive oil
1 shallot, chopped finely
2 garlic cloves, crushed
1 lb 2 oz/500 g canned chopped tomatoes
1 tbsp chopped fresh basil
salt and pepper

**NUTRITION**
Calories *592*; Sugars *6 g*; Protein *28 g*; Carbohydrate *57 g*; Fat *29 g*; Saturates *17 g*

 easy

15 mins

35–40 mins

# Fish *and* Seafood

The range of seafood available these days is immense, but sometimes it is difficult to know how to cook unfamiliar fish. The answer might be to put it in a pot and make a fabulous stew. Jambalaya (see page 156), Italian Fish Stew (see page 157) or Bouillabaisse (see page 159) are as different as their countries of origin, equally delicious and incredibly easy to make. Another answer might be to stir it with rice to make an elegant Crab Risotto (see page 170) or to combine it with chillies and other spices in a one-pot Thai Green Fish Curry (see page 154). Then again, there are soups and chowders, bakes and pasta dishes. There are recipes for inexpensive family meals and dishes for sophisticated entertaining, featuring seafood of all kinds from cod to shrimp and from sardines to squid—even a lobster one-pot.

This is a traditional, creamy soup from Scotland. As the smoked haddock has quite a strong flavor, it has been mixed with some cod.

# Cullen Skink

**SERVES 4**

8 oz/225 g undyed smoked haddock fillet
2 tbsp butter
1 onion, chopped finely
2½ cups milk
2¼ cups diced potatoes
12 oz/350 g cod, boned, skinned and cubed
⅔ cup heavy cream
2 tbsp chopped fresh parsley
lemon juice, to taste
salt and pepper

*to garnish*
lemon slices
sprigs of fresh parsley

1  Put the haddock fillet in a large skillet and cover with boiling water. Let stand for 10 minutes. Drain, reserving 1¼ cups of the soaking water. Flake the fish and remove all the bones.

2  Heat the butter in a large pan and add the onion. Cook gently for 10 minutes until softened. Add the milk and bring to a gentle simmer before adding the potatoes. Cook for 10 minutes.

3  Add the reserved haddock flakes and cod. Simmer for an additional 10 minutes until the cod is tender.

4  Remove about one third of the fish and potatoes, put in a food processor, and blend until smooth. Alternatively, push the mixture through a strainer into a bowl. Return to the soup with the cream, parsley, and seasoning. Taste and add a little lemon juice, if desired. Add a little of the reserved soaking water if the soup seems too thick. Reheat gently and serve the soup immediately, garnished with parsley and lemon slices.

**NUTRITION**

Calories *108*; Sugars *2.3 g*; Protein *7.4 g*;
Carbohydrate *5.6 g*; Fat *6.4 g*; Saturates *4 g*

 moderate

 20 mins

20 mins

40 mins

 **COOK'S TIP**

Always try to find undyed smoked haddock, or, even better Finnan haddock. Do not use yellow-dyed haddock fillet, which is often whiting and not actually haddock at all.

Juicy chunks of fish and sumptuous shellfish are cooked in a flavorful bouillon. Serve with toasted bread rubbed with garlic.

# Mediterranean Fish Soup

1 Heat the olive oil in a large, heavy-based saucepan and gently fry the onion and garlic for 2–3 minutes, until just softened.

2 Pour in the bouillon and wine and bring to a boil.

3 Tie the bay leaf and herbs together with clean string and add to the saucepan with the fish and mussels. Stir well, cover, and simmer for 5 minutes.

4 Stir in the tomatoes and shrimp and continue to cook for another 3–4 minutes, until piping hot and the fish is cooked through.

5 Discard the herbs and any mussels that have not opened. Season with salt and pepper to taste, then ladle into warm soup bowls.

6 Garnish with sprigs of fresh thyme and serve with lemon wedges and toasted bread rubbed with garlic.

SERVES 4

1 tbsp olive oil
1 large onion, chopped
2 garlic cloves, chopped finely
1¾ cups Fresh Fish Bouillon (see page 14)
⅔ cup dry white wine
1 bay leaf
1 sprig each of fresh thyme, rosemary, and oregano
1 lb/450 g firm white fish fillets, such as cod, angler fish, or halibut, skinned and cut into 1-inch/2.5-cm cubes
1 lb/450 g fresh mussels, prepared
14 oz/400 g canned chopped tomatoes
8 oz/225 g peeled, cooked shrimp, thawed if frozen
salt and pepper
sprigs of fresh thyme, to garnish

*to serve*
lemon wedges
4 slices toasted French bread, rubbed with a cut garlic clove

NUTRITION
Calories 316; Sugars 4 g; Protein 53 g; Carbohydrate 5 g; Fat 7 g; Saturates 1 g

⭐⭐⭐ moderate
🕐 1 hr
🕐 15 mins

Any mixture of fish is suitable for this recipe, from simple smoked and white fish to salmon or mussels, depending on the occasion.

# Mixed Fish Soup

**SERVES 4**

2 tbsp vegetable oil
1 lb/450 g small new potatoes, halved
1 bunch scallions, sliced
1 yellow bell pepper, sliced
2 garlic cloves, crushed
1 cup dry white wine
2½ cups fish bouillon
8 oz/225 g white fish fillet, skinned and cubed
8 oz/225 g smoked cod fillet, skinned and cubed
2 tomatoes, peeled, seeded, and chopped
1 cup peeled cooked shrimp
⅔ cup heavy cream
2 tbsp shredded fresh basil

1 Heat the vegetable oil in a large pan and add the potatoes, sliced scallions, bell pepper, and garlic. Sauté gently for 3 minutes, stirring constantly.

2 Add the white wine and fish bouillon to the pan and bring to a boil. Reduce the heat and simmer the mixture for about 10–15 minutes.

3 Add the cubed fish fillets and the tomatoes to the soup and continue to cook for 10 minutes or until the fish is cooked through.

4 Stir in the shrimp, cream, and shredded basil and cook for 2–3 minutes. Pour the soup into warmed bowls and serve immediately.

**NUTRITION**
Calories *458*; Sugars *5 g*; Protein *28 g*;
Carbohydrate *22 g*; Fat *25 g*; Saturates *12 g*

 easy

 10 mins

 35 mins

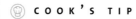 **COOK'S TIP**

For a soup that is slightly less rich, omit the wine and stir plain yogurt into the soup instead of the heavy cream.

This soup is also known as Tom Yam Gung. Asian stores may sell ready-prepared tom yam sauce in jars, sometimes labeled "Chiles in Oil."

# Thai Fish Soup

1 First make the tom yam sauce. Heat the oil in a small skillet. Cook the garlic for a few seconds until just brown. Remove with a draining spoon and set aside. Cook the shallot in the oil until browned and crisp, add the chiles, and cook until they darken. Remove and drain on paper towels. Remove the pan from the stove and save the oil for later use.

2 In a food processor or a spice grinder, grind the dried shrimp, if using, then the reserved chiles, garlic, and shallot to a smooth paste. Return to the original pan over low heat. Mix in the fish sauce and sugar. Remove from the heat.

3 In a large pan, heat together the bouillon and 2 tablespoons of the tom yam sauce. Add the lime leaves, lemongrass, lemon juice, fish sauce, chiles, and sugar. Simmer for 2 minutes.

4 Add the mushrooms and shrimp, and cook for another 2–3 minutes until the shrimp are cooked. Ladle into warm bowls and serve immediately, garnished with the shredded scallions.

SERVES 4

2 cups light chicken bouillon
2 lime leaves, chopped
2-inch/5-cm piece lemongrass, chopped
3 tbsp lemon juice
3 tbsp Thai fish sauce
2 small, hot green chiles, seeded and chopped finely
½ tsp sugar
8 small shiitake mushrooms, halved
1 lb/450 g raw shrimp, peeled if necessary and deveined
scallions (shredded), to garnish

*tom yam sauce*

4 tbsp vegetable oil
5 garlic cloves, chopped finely
1 large shallot, chopped finely
2 large hot dried red chiles, chopped coarsely
1 tbsp dried shrimp (optional)
1 tbsp Thai fish sauce
2 tsp sugar

**NUTRITION**
Calories 230; Sugars 4 g; Protein 22 g;
Carbohydrate 9 g; Fat 12 g; Saturates 1 g

⭐⭐⭐ moderate
 25 mins
 5 mins

This soup is based on the classic Chinese chicken and corn soup, but the delicate flavor of the crab works very well.

# Chinese Crab *and* Corn Soup

**SERVES 4**

1 tbsp vegetable oil
1 small onion, chopped finely
1 garlic clove, chopped finely
1 tsp grated fresh gingerroot
1 small red chile, seeded and chopped finely
2 tbsp dry sherry or Chinese rice wine
8 oz/225 g fresh white crab meat
1½ cups canned corn, drained
1 pint/600 ml light chicken bouillon
1 tbsp light soy sauce
2 tbsp chopped fresh cilantro
2 eggs, beaten
salt and pepper
chile "flowers," to garnish

1 Heat the oil in a large saucepan and add the onion. Cook gently for 5 minutes until softened. Add the garlic, gingerroot and chile and cook for another minute.

2 Add the sherry or rice wine and bubble until reduced by half. Add the crab meat, corn, chicken bouillon, and soy sauce. Bring to a boil and simmer gently for 5 minutes. Stir in the cilantro. Season to taste.

3 Remove from the heat and pour in the eggs. Wait for a few seconds and then stir well, to break the eggs into ribbons. Serve the soup immediately, garnished with chile "flowers."

**NUTRITION**
Calories 248; Sugars 8 g; Protein 18 g;
Carbohydrate 20 g; Fat 10 g; Saturates 2 g

easy

10 mins

15 mins

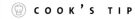 **COOK'S TIP**

For convenience, you could use canned crab meat. Make sure it is well drained before adding it to the soup.

This recipe is intended to be served in small quantities, because the soup is very rich and full of flavor.

# Clam *and* Sorrel Soup

1 Put the clams in a large pan with the onion and wine. Cover and cook over high heat for 3–4 minutes until the clams have opened. Strain, reserving the cooking liquid, but discarding the onion. Set aside the clams until they are cool enough to handle.

2 In a clean pan, melt the butter over low heat. Add the carrot, shallots, and celery, and cook them very gently for 10 minutes until softened but not colored. Add the reserved cooking liquid and bay leaves and simmer the soup for an additional 10 minutes.

3 Meanwhile, coarsely chop the clams, if large. Add to the soup with the cream and sorrel. Simmer for another 2–3 minutes until the sorrel has collapsed. Season with pepper and serve immediately with crusty bread.

**SERVES 4**

2 lb/900 g live clams, scrubbed
1 onion, chopped finely
⅔ cup dry white wine
4 tbsp butter
1 small carrot, diced finely
2 shallots, diced finely
1 celery stalk, diced finely
2 bay leaves
⅔ cup heavy cream
1 cup loosely packed shredded sorrel
pepper
crusty bread, to serve
dill, to garnish

**NUTRITION**
Calories *348*; Sugars *5 g*; Protein *10 g*; Carbohydrate *7 g*; Fat *29 g*; Saturates *18 g*

easy

20 mins

30 mins

 **COOK'S TIP**

Sorrel is a large-leafed herb with a slightly sour, lemony flavor that goes very well with fish. It is increasingly easy to find in larger supermarkets, but is also incredibly easy to grow.

Packed full of flavor, this delicious fish dish is really a meal in itself, but it is ideal accompanied by a crisp side salad.

# Fish *and* Crab Chowder

**SERVES 4**

1 large onion, chopped finely
2 celery stalks, chopped finely
²/₃ cup dry white wine
2¹/₂ cups fish bouillon
2¹/₂ cups skim milk
1 bay leaf
8 oz/225 g smoked cod fillet, skinned and cut into 1-inch/2.5-cm cubes
8 oz/225 g smoked haddock fillets, skinned and cut into 1-inch/2.5-cm cubes
12 oz/350 g canned crab meat, drained
2 cups blanched green beans, sliced into 1-inch/2.5-cm pieces
1¹/₃ cups cooked brown rice
4 tsp cornstarch mixed with 4 tbsp water
salt and pepper
chopped fresh parsley to garnish
mixed salad greens, to serve

1 Place the onion, celery, and wine in a large nonstick pan. Bring to a boil, cover, and cook over low heat for 5 minutes.

2 Uncover the pan and cook for another 5 minutes until almost all the liquid has evaporated.

3 Pour in the bouillon and milk and add the bay leaf. Bring to a simmer and stir in the cod and haddock. Simmer over low heat, uncovered, for 5 minutes.

4 Add the crab meat, beans, and cooked brown rice and simmer gently for 2–3 minutes until just heated through. Remove the bay leaf with a draining spoon and discard.

5 Stir in the cornstarch mixture until thickened slightly. Season to taste with salt and pepper and ladle into warmed soup bowls. Garnish with chopped parsley and serve with a mixed salad.

**NUTRITION**
Calories *440*; Sugars *10 g*; Protein *49 g*;
Carbohydrate *43 g*; Fat *7 g*; Saturates *1 g*

easy

40 mins

25 mins

In Spain, giant garlic shrimp are cooked in small half-glazed earthenware dishes called *cazuelas*. The shrimp arrive at your table sizzling.

# Giant Garlic Shrimp

1 Heat the oil in a large, heavy skillet over low heat. Add the garlic and chiles and cook, stirring occasionally, for 1–2 minutes until softened, but not colored.

2 Add the shrimp and stir-fry for 2–3 minutes until heated through and coated in the oil and garlic mixture.

3 Turn off the heat and add the chopped fresh flatleaf parsley, stirring well to mix. Season to taste with salt and pepper.

4 Divide the shrimp and garlic-flavored oil among warmed serving dishes and serve with lots of crusty bread. Garnish with lemon wedges.

**SERVES 4**

½ cup olive oil
4 garlic cloves, chopped finely
2 hot fresh red chiles, seeded and chopped finely
1 lb/450 g cooked jumbo shrimp
2 tbsp chopped fresh flatleaf parsley
salt and pepper
lemon wedges, to garnish
crusty bread, to serve

**NUTRITION**
Calories 385; Sugars 0 g; Protein 26 g; Carbohydrate 1 g; Fat 31 g; Saturates 5 g

 very easy

 5 mins

 5–8 mins

**COOK'S TIP**

If you can get hold of raw shrimp, cook them as above but increase the cooking time to 5–6 minutes until the shrimp are cooked through and turn bright pink. If using frozen shrimp, make sure they are thoroughly thawed before cooking.

This souplike entrée rice dish is packed with a tempting array of fresh seafood and is typically Thai in flavor.

# Rice *with* Seafood

**SERVES 4**

12 live mussels, scrubbed and bearded
8¾ cups fish bouillon
2 tbsp vegetable oil
1 garlic clove, crushed
1 tsp grated fresh gingerroot
1 fresh red bird's-eye chile, chopped
2 scallions, chopped
generous 1 cup long-grain rice
2 small squid, cleaned and sliced
3½ oz/100 g firm white fish fillet, such as halibut or angler fish, cut into chunks
1 cup peeled raw shrimp
2 tbsp Thai fish sauce
3 tbsp chopped fresh cilantro

1 Discard any mussels with damaged shells or open ones that do not close when firmly tapped with a knife. Pour 4 tablespoons of the bouillon into a large pan. Add the mussels, cover, and cook over medium heat, shaking the pan until the mussels open. Remove from the heat and discard any which have failed to open.

2 Heat the oil in a large skillet or wok and stir-fry the garlic, gingerroot, chile, and scallions for 30 seconds. Add the remaining bouillon and bring to a boil.

3 Stir in the rice, then add the squid, fish chunks, and shrimp. Lower the heat and simmer gently for 15 minutes or until the rice is cooked. Add the fish sauce and mussels.

4 Ladle into wide bowls and sprinkle with chopped cilantro before serving.

**NUTRITION**
Calories *370*; Sugars *0 g*; Protein *27 g*; Carbohydrate *52 g*; Fat *8 g*; Saturates *1 g*

 moderate

5–10 mins

20 mins

 **COOK'S TIP**

You could use leftover cooked rice for this dish. Just simmer the seafood gently until cooked, then stir in the rice at the end.

The sweet briny flesh of shrimp is wonderful paired with the smoky scent of chipotle chiles.

# Shrimp *in* Green Sauce

1 Heat the oil in a large pan. Add the onions and garlic and cook over low heat, stirring occasionally, for about 5–10 minutes until softened. Add the tomatoes and cook for 2 minutes.

2 Add the green beans, cumin, allspice, cinnamon, chipotle chile and marinade, and fish bouillon. Bring to a boil, then reduce the heat, and simmer for a few minutes to combine the flavors.

3 Add the shrimp and cook, stirring gently, for 1–2 minutes only, then remove the pan from the heat and set the shrimp aside to steep in the hot liquid to finish cooking. They are cooked when they have turned a bright pink color.

4 Serve the shrimp immediately, garnished with the fresh cilantro, and accompanied by the lime wedges.

**SERVES 4**

2 tbsp vegetable oil

3 onions, chopped

5 garlic cloves, chopped

5–7 ripe tomatoes, diced

1½–2 cups green beans, cut into 2-inch/5-cm pieces and blanched for 1 minute

¼ tsp ground cumin

pinch of ground allspice

pinch of ground cinnamon

½–1 canned chipotle chile in adobo marinade, with some of the marinade

2 cups fish bouillon or water mixed with a fish bouillon cube

1 lb/450 g raw shrimp, peeled

sprigs of fresh cilantro

1 lime, cut into wedges

**NUTRITION**
Calories *225*; Sugars *13 g*; Protein *24 g*; Carbohydrate *17 g*; Fat *8 g*; Saturates *1 g*

   easy

  10 mins

15–20 mins

 **COOK'S TIP**

If you can find them, use bottled nopales (edible cacti), cut into strips, to add an exotic touch to the dish.

A Thai-influenced dish of rice, cooked in coconut milk, with spicy broiled angler fish and fresh peas.

# Spicy Angler Fish Rice

**S E R V E S  4**

1 hot red chile, seeded and chopped
1 tsp chili flakes
2 garlic cloves, chopped
2 pinches of saffron
3 tbsp coarsely chopped mint leaves
4 tbsp olive oil
2 tbsp lemon juice
12 oz/350 g angler fish fillet, cut into bite-size pieces
1 onion, chopped finely
1 cup long-grain rice
14 oz/400 g canned chopped tomatoes
³⁄₄ cup coconut milk
1 cup peas
salt and pepper
2 tbsp chopped fresh cilantro, to garnish

1 In a food processor or blender, blend the fresh and dried chile, garlic, saffron, mint, olive oil, and lemon juice until finely chopped but not smooth.

2 Put the angler fish into a nonmetallic dish and pour over the spice paste, mixing together well. Set aside for 20 minutes to marinate.

3 Heat a large pan until it is very hot. Using a draining spoon, lift the angler fish from the marinade and add, in batches, to the hot pan. Cook for 3–4 minutes until browned and firm. Remove with a draining spoon and set aside while you cook the rice.

4 Add the onion and remaining marinade to the same pan and cook for 5 minutes until softened and lightly browned. Add the rice and stir until well coated. Add the tomatoes and coconut milk. Bring to a boil, cover, and simmer very gently for 15 minutes. Stir in the peas, season, and arrange the fish over the top. Cover with foil and continue to cook over very low heat for 5 minutes. Serve garnished with the chopped cilantro.

**N U T R I T I O N**
Calories *440*; Sugars *8 g*; Protein *22 g*; Carbohydrate *60 g*; Fat *14 g*; Saturates *2 g*

easy

30 mins

30 mins

This flavorful squid dish from Vera Cruz in Mexico would be good with warmed flour tortillas, for do-it-yourself tacos.

# Simmered Squid

1 Heat the oil in a pan and lightly fry the squid until it turns opaque. Season with salt and pepper and remove from the pan with a draining spoon.

2 Add the onion and garlic to the remaining oil in the pan and cook until softened. Stir in the tomatoes, chile, herbs, cinnamon, allspice, sugar, and olives. Cover and cook over medium-low heat for 5–10 minutes until the mixture thickens slightly. Uncover the pan and cook for another 5 minutes to concentrate the flavors and reduce the liquid.

3 Stir in the reserved squid and any of the juices that have gathered. Add the capers and heat through.

4 Adjust the seasoning if necessary, then serve, garnished with fresh cilantro.

SERVES 4

3 tbsp extra virgin olive oil
2 lb/900 g cleaned squid, cut into rings and tentacles
1 onion, chopped
3 garlic cloves, chopped
14 oz/400 g canned chopped tomatoes
1/2–1 fresh mild green chile, seeded and chopped
1 tbsp chopped finely fresh parsley
1/4 tsp chopped fresh thyme
1/4 tsp chopped fresh oregano
1/4 tsp chopped fresh marjoram
pinch of ground cinnamon
pinch of ground allspice
pinch of sugar
15–20 pimiento-stuffed green olives, sliced
1 tbsp capers
salt and pepper
1 tbsp chopped fresh cilantro, to garnish

**NUTRITION**
Calories 307; Sugars 6 g; Protein 36 g;
Carbohydrate 10 g; Fat 14 g; Saturates 2 g

 easy

 10 mins

 20 mins

This is a modern version of the classic dish, using smoked salmon as well as fresh salmon and lots of fresh herbs.

# A Modern Kedgeree

## SERVES 4

2 tbsp butter
1 tbsp olive oil
1 onion, chopped finely
1 garlic clove, chopped finely
1 scant cup long-grain rice
1²⁄₃ cups fish bouillon
6 oz/175 g skinless, boneless salmon fillet, chopped
3 oz/85 g smoked salmon, chopped
2 tbsp heavy cream
2 tbsp chopped fresh dill
3 scallions, chopped finely
salt and pepper

*to garnish*
lemon slices
sprigs of fresh dill

1 Melt the butter with the oil in a large pan. Add the onion and cook gently for 10 minutes until softened but not colored. Add the garlic and cook for another 30 seconds.

2 Add the rice to the pan and cook for 2–3 minutes, stirring, until transparent. Add the fish bouillon and stir well. Bring to a boil, cover, and simmer very gently for 10 minutes.

3 Add the salmon fillet and the smoked salmon and stir well, adding a little more bouillon or water if it seems dry. Return to the heat and cook for another 6–8 minutes until the fish and rice are tender and all the bouillon has been absorbed.

4 Remove from the heat and stir in the cream, dill, and scallions. Season to taste and serve, garnished with a sprig of dill and slice of lemon.

## NUTRITION

Calories *370*; Sugars *3 g*; Protein *10 g*; Carbohydrate *39 g*; Fat *190 g*; Saturates *9 g*

easy

10 mins

35 mins

### COOK'S TIP

Use smoked salmon trimmings for a budget dish.

An unusual and striking dish with fresh shrimp and asparagus, which is very simple to prepare and ideal for impromptu supper parties.

# Shrimp *and* Asparagus Risotto

1 Bring the vegetable bouillon to a boil in a large pan. Add the asparagus and cook for 3 minutes until just tender. Strain, reserving the bouillon, and refresh the asparagus under cold running water. Drain and set aside.

2 Heat the olive oil in a large skillet, add the onion, and cook gently for 5 minutes until softened. Add the garlic and cook for another 30 seconds. Add the rice and stir for 1–2 minutes until coated with oil and slightly translucent.

3 Keep the vegetable bouillon over low heat. Increase the heat under the rice to medium and begin adding the bouillon, 1 cup at a time, stirring well between additions. Continue until almost all the bouillon has been absorbed. This should take 20–25 minutes.

4 Add the shrimp and asparagus, with the last cup of vegetable bouillon, and cook for 5 minutes until the shrimp and rice are tender and the bouillon has been absorbed. Remove from the heat.

5 Stir in the olive paste, basil, and seasoning, and let stand for 1 minute. Serve immediately, garnished with Parmesan shavings.

**SERVES  4**

5 cups vegetable bouillon
12 oz/350 g asparagus, cut into
   2-inch/5-cm lengths
2 tbsp olive oil
1 onion, chopped finely
1 garlic clove, chopped finely
1½ cups arborio rice
1 lb/450 g raw jumbo shrimp, peeled
   and deveined
2 tbsp olive paste or tapenade
2 tbsp chopped fresh basil
salt and pepper
Parmesan cheese shavings, to garnish

**NUTRITION**
Calories *566*; Sugars *4 g*; Protein *30 g*;
Carbohydrate *86 g*; Fat *14 g*; Saturates *2 g*

   moderate

   10 mins

   40 mins

Fusilli, corkscrew-shaped pasta, is the best shape to use for this recipe because the creamy sauce is absorbed in the twists.

# Pasta *with* Tuna *and* Lemon

**SERVES 4**

4 tbsp butter, diced
1¼ cups heavy cream
4 tbsp lemon juice
1 tbsp grated lemon rind
½ tsp anchovy extract
14 oz/400 g dried fusilli
7 oz/200 g canned tuna in olive oil, drained and flaked
salt and pepper

*to garnish*
2 tbsp chopped finely fresh parsley
strips of lemon rind

1 Bring a large saucepan of lightly salted water to a boil. Cook the pasta for 10–12 minutes or according to the instructions on the package until tender but firm to the bite. Drain.

2 To make the sauce, melt the butter in a large skillet. Stir in the heavy cream and lemon juice and simmer, stirring, for approximately 2 minutes, or until slightly thickened. Stir in the grated lemon rind and anchovy extract.

3 Drain the pasta well. Add the pasta sauce and toss until well coated. Add the tuna and gently toss until well blended but not too broken up.

4 Season with salt and pepper. Transfer to a serving platter and garnish with the parsley and lemon rind. Grind over some pepper and serve at once.

**NUTRITION**
Calories *892*; Sugars *5 g*; Protein *27 g*; Carbohydrate *78 g*; Fat *55 g*; Saturates *32 g*

easy

10 mins

15 mins

🍳 **COOK'S TIP**

For a vegetarian version, omit the tuna and anchovy extract. Add 5 oz/150 g pitted olives instead. For extra "kick" add a pinch of dried chili flakes to the sauce instead of the anchovy extract.

Mussels cooked in beer, tomatoes, and Mexican spices are great summertime fare.

# Mussels Cooked *with* Beer

1 Scrub the mussels under cold running water to remove any mud. Using a sharp knife, cut away the feathery "beards" from the shells. Discard any open mussels that do not shut when tapped sharply with a knife. Rinse again under cold water.

2 Place the beer, onions, garlic, chile, and tomatoes in a heavy-based pan. Bring to a boil.

3 Add the mussels and cook, covered, over medium-high heat for about 10 minutes until the shells open. Discard any mussels that do not open.

4 Ladle into individual bowls and serve sprinkled with fresh cilantro.

**SERVES 4**

1.5 kg/3 lb 5 oz live mussels
2 cups beer
2 onions, chopped
5 garlic cloves, chopped coarsely
1 fresh green chile, such as jalapeño or serrano, deseeded and sliced thinly
6 oz/175 g fresh tomatoes, diced, or canned chopped
2–3 tbsp chopped fresh cilantro

**NUTRITION**
Calories *144*; Sugars *8 g*; Protein *13 g*; Carbohydrate *12 g*; Fat *2 g*; Saturates *0.25 g*

  COOK'S TIP

Add the kernels of 2 corn-on-the- cob to the beer mixture at Step 2. A pinch of sugar might be needed to bring out the sweetness of the corn.

⭐⭐ easy

🕐 35 mins

🕐 15 mins

These delicious large mussels are served hot with a tasty tomato and vegetable sauce. Mop up the delicious sauce with some crusty bread.

# Provençale-Style Mussels

**SERVES 4**

1 tbsp olive oil

1 large onion, chopped finely

1 garlic clove, chopped finely

1 small red bell pepper, seeded and chopped finely

1 fresh rosemary sprig

2 bay leaves

400 g/14 oz canned chopped tomatoes

²⁄₃ cup white wine

1 zucchini, diced finely

2 tbsp tomato paste

1 tsp superfine sugar

½ pitted black olives in brine, drained and chopped

1½ lb/675 g cooked New Zealand green mussels in their shells

1 tsp grated orange rind

salt and pepper

crusty bread, to serve

2 tbsp chopped fresh parsley, to garnish

1 Heat the olive oil in a large saucepan and gently fry the chopped onion, garlic, and bell pepper for 3–4 minutes until just softened.

2 Add the rosemary and bay leaves to the saucepan with the tomatoes and ⅓ cup wine. Season to taste, then bring to a boil and simmer for 15 minutes.

3 Stir in the zucchini, tomato paste, sugar, and olives. Simmer for 10 minutes.

4 Meanwhile, bring a pan of water to a boil. Arrange the mussels in a steamer or a large strainer and place over the water. Sprinkle with the remaining wine and the orange rind. Cover and steam until the mussels open (discard any that remain closed).

5 Remove the mussels with a draining spoon and arrange on a serving plate. Discard the herbs and spoon the sauce over the mussels. Garnish with chopped parsley and serve with crusty bread.

**NUTRITION**

Calories 253; Sugars 8 g; Protein 31 g; Carbohydrate 9 g; Fat 8 g; Saturates 1 g

 challenging

5 mins

50 mins

The fish in this fragrant, currylike stew can be varied according to taste or availability, but do choose ones that stay firm when cooked.

# Spicy Thai Seafood Stew

1 Cut the squid body cavities into thick rings and cut the fish fillet into bite-size chunks.

2 Heat the oil in a large skillet or wok and stir-fry the shallots, garlic, and curry paste for 1–2 minutes. Add the lemongrass and shrimp paste, stir in the coconut milk, and bring to a boil.

3 Reduce the heat to low. When the liquid is simmering gently, add the white fish chunks, squid rings, and jumbo shrimp to the skillet or wok. Stir and then simmer for 2 minutes.

4 Add the clams and simmer for another minute until the clams open. Discard any clams that do not open.

5 Sprinkle the shredded basil leaves over the stew and serve immediately, garnished with whole basil leaves and spooned over boiled rice.

**SERVES 4**

½ lb/225 g prepared squid

1 lb 2 oz/450 g firm white fish fillet, preferably angler fish or halibut

1 tbsp sunflower oil

4 shallots, chopped finely

2 garlic cloves, chopped finely

2 tbsp Thai green curry paste

2 small lemongrass stalks, chopped finely

1 tsp shrimp paste

2¼ cups coconut milk

8 oz/225 g raw jumbo shrimp, peeled and deveined

12 live clams, scrubbed

8 fresh basil leaves, shredded finely, plus extra to garnish

boiled rice, to serve

**NUTRITION**
Calories 267; Sugars 7 g; Protein 42 g; Carbohydrate 9 g; Fat 7 g; Saturates 1 g

 moderate

5 mins

10 mins

## COOK'S TIP

If you prefer, fresh mussels in shells can be used instead of clams—add them at Step 4 and follow the recipe.

This pale-green curry paste can be used as the basis for all sorts of Thai dishes. It is also delicious with chicken and beef.

# Thai Green Fish Curry

**SERVES 4**

2 tbsp vegetable oil
1 garlic clove, chopped
1 small eggplant, diced
½ cup coconut cream
2 tbsp Thai fish sauce
1 tsp sugar
8 oz/225 g firm white fish, cut into pieces,
    such as cod, haddock, or halibut
½ cup fish bouillon
2 kaffir lime leaves, shredded finely
about 15 leaves Thai basil, or ordinary basil
plain boiled rice or noodles, to serve

*green curry paste*
5 fresh green chiles, seeded and chopped
2 tsp chopped lemongrass
1 large shallot, chopped
2 garlic cloves, chopped
1 tsp grated fresh gingerroot or galangal
2 sprigs of fresh cilantro, chopped
½ tsp ground coriander
¼ tsp ground cumin
1 kaffir lime leaf, chopped finely
½ tsp salt

**NUTRITION**
Calories 217; Sugars 3 g; Protein 12 g;
Carbohydrate 5 g; Fat 17 g; Saturates 10 g

easy

15 mins

15 mins

1 Make the curry paste. Put all the ingredients into a blender or spice grinder and blend to a smooth paste, adding a little water if necessary. Alternatively, pound together all the ingredients, using a mortar and pestle, until smooth. Set the curry paste aside.

2 Heat the oil in a skillet or wok until almost smoking. Add the garlic and fry until golden. Add the curry paste and stir-fry for a few seconds before adding the eggplant. Stir-fry for about 4–5 minutes until softened.

3 Add the coconut cream. Bring to a boil and stir until the cream thickens and curdles slightly. Add the fish sauce and sugar and stir into the mixture.

4 Add the fish pieces and bouillon. Simmer, stirring occasionally, for 3–4 minutes until the fish is just tender. Add the lime leaves and basil and then cook for another 1 minute.

5 Transfer to a warmed serving dish and serve with boiled rice or noodles.

Goan cuisine is famous for seafood and vindaloo dishes, which tend to be very hot. This recipe is a mild curry, but very flavorful.

# Goan Fish Curry

1 Put the fish on a plate and drizzle the vinegar over it. Combine half the salt and half the turmeric and sprinkle evenly over the fish. Cover and set aside for 20 minutes.

2 Heat the oil in a heavy skillet and add the garlic. Brown slightly, then add the onion, and cook, stirring occasionally, for 3–4 minutes until soft, but not browned. Add the ground coriander and stir for 1 minute.

3 Mix the remaining turmeric, cayenne, and paprika with about 2 tablespoons water to make a paste. Add to the skillet and cook over low heat for 1–2 minutes.

4 Stir the tamarind pulp and boiling water. When thickened and the pulp has come away from the seeds, rub through a strainer. Discard the seeds.

5 Add the coconut, warm water, and tamarind paste to the skillet and stir until the coconut has dissolved. Add the fish and any juices on the plate and simmer gently for 4–5 minutes until the sauce has thickened and the fish is just tender. Serve on a bed of plain boiled rice.

**SERVES 4**

1¾ lb/785 g angler fish fillet, cut into chunks
1 tbsp cider vinegar
1 tsp salt
1 tsp ground turmeric
3 tbsp vegetable oil
2 garlic cloves, crushed
1 small onion, chopped finely
2 tsp ground coriander
1 tsp cayenne pepper
2 tsp paprika
2 tbsp tamarind pulp plus 2 tbsp boiling water (see Step 4)
¾ cup creamed coconut, cut into pieces
1¼ cups warm water
plain boiled rice, to serve

**NUTRITION**
Calories *302*; Sugars *7 g*; Protein *31 g*; Carbohydrate *8 g*; Fat *17 g*; Saturates *7 g*

★★      easy

      30 mins

      15 mins

Jambalaya is a dish of Cajun origin. There are as many versions of this dish as there are people who cook it. Here is a straightforward one.

# Jambalaya

## SERVES 4

2 tbsp vegetable oil
2 onions, chopped coarsely
1 green bell pepper, seeded and chopped coarsely
2 celery stalks, chopped coarsely
3 garlic cloves, chopped finely
2 tsp paprika
10½ oz/300 g skinless, boneless chicken breast portions, chopped
4 oz/100 g kabanos sausages, chopped
3 tomatoes, peeled and chopped
2¼ cups long-grain rice
3¾ cups hot chicken or fish bouillon
1 tsp dried oregano
2 bay leaves
12 large shrimp tails
4 scallions, chopped finely
2 tbsp chopped fresh parsley
salt and pepper
salad, to serve

## NUTRITION
Calories 283; Sugars 8 g; Protein 30 g; Carbohydrate 12 g; Fat 14 g; Saturates 3 g

  easy

  10 mins

  45 mins

1 Heat the vegetable oil in a large skillet and add the onions, bell pepper, celery, and garlic. Cook over low heat, stirring occasionally, for about 8–10 minutes until all the vegetables have softened. Add the paprika and cook for another 30 seconds. Add the chicken and sausages and cook for 8–10 minutes until lightly browned. Add the tomatoes and cook for 2–3 minutes until collapsed.

2 Add the rice to the pan and stir well. Pour in the hot bouillon and stir in the oregano and bay leaves. Cover and simmer for 10 minutes over low heat.

3 Add the shrimp and stir well. Cover again and cook for another 6–8 minutes until the rice is tender and the shrimp are cooked through.

4 Stir in the scallions and parsley and season to taste. Serve with salad.

### COOK'S TIP

Jambalaya is a versatile dish which has some basic ingredients—onions, green bell peppers, celery, rice, and seasonings—to which you can add whatever else you may have to hand.

This robust stew is full of Mediterranean flavors. If you do not want to prepare the fish yourself, ask your local fish store to do it for you.

# Italian Fish Stew

1 Heat the oil in a large pan. Add the onions and garlic and cook over low heat, stirring occasionally, for about 5 minutes until softened. Add the zucchini and cook, stirring frequently, for 2–3 minutes.

2 Add the tomatoes and bouillon to the pan and bring to a boil. Add the pasta, bring back to a boil, reduce the heat, and cover. Simmer for 5 minutes.

3 Skin and bone the fish, then cut it into chunks. Add to the pan with the basil or oregano and lemon rind and simmer gently for 5 minutes until the fish is opaque and flakes easily (take care not to overcook it) and the pasta is tender, but still firm to the bite.

4 Blend the cornstarch with the water to a smooth paste and stir into the stew. Cook gently for 2 minutes, stirring constantly, until thickened. Season with salt and pepper to taste.

5 Ladle the stew into 4 warmed soup bowls. Garnish with basil or oregano sprigs and serve immediately.

**SERVES 4**

2 tbsp olive oil
2 red onions, chopped finely
1 garlic clove, crushed
2 zucchini, sliced
14 oz/400 g canned chopped tomatoes
3¾ cups fish or vegetable bouillon
¾ cup dried pasta shapes
12 oz/350 g firm white fish, such as cod, haddock, or hake
1 tbsp chopped fresh basil or oregano or 1 tsp dried oregano
1 tsp grated lemon rind
1 tbsp cornstarch
1 tbsp water
salt and pepper
sprigs of fresh basil or oregano, to garnish

**NUTRITION**
Calories *236*; Sugars *4 g*; Protein *20 g*; Carbohydrate *25 g*; Fat *7 g*; Saturates *1 g*

moderate

5–10 mins

25 mins

This is a rich French stew of fish and vegetables, flavored with saffron and herbs. The fish and vegetables, and the soup, are served separately.

# Cotriade

**SERVES 4**

pinch of saffron
2½ cups hot fish bouillon
1 tbsp olive oil
2 tbsp butter
1 onion, sliced
2 garlic cloves, chopped
1 leek, sliced
1 small fennel bulb, sliced thinly
1 lb/450 g potatoes, cut into chunks
⅔ cup dry white wine
1 tbsp fresh thyme leaves
2 bay leaves
4 ripe tomatoes, peeled and chopped
2 lb/900 g mixed fish fillets, such as
  haddock, hake, mackerel, or red mullet,
  coarsely chopped
2 tbsp chopped fresh parsley
salt and pepper
crusty bread, to serve

1 Using a mortar and pestle, crush the saffron and add it to the fish bouillon. Stir the mixture and set aside to infuse for at least 10 minutes.

2 Heat the olive oil and butter together in a large, heavy pan. Add the onion and cook over low heat, stirring occasionally, for 4–5 minutes until softened, but not browned. Add the garlic, leek, fennel, and potatoes. Cover and cook for another 10–15 minutes until the vegetables are softened.

3 Add the white wine and simmer rapidly for 3–4 minutes until it has reduced by about half. Add the thyme, bay leaves, and tomatoes and stir well. Add the saffron-steeped fish bouillon. Bring to a boil, cover, and simmer over low heat for about 15 minutes until all the vegetables are tender.

4 Add the fish, return to a boil, and simmer for a further 3–4 minutes until all the fish is tender. Add the parsley and season to taste. Using a draining spoon, transfer the fish and vegetables to a warmed serving dish. Serve the soup with plenty of crusty bread.

**NUTRITION**
Calories 81; Sugars 1 g; Protein 7.4 g;
Carbohydrate 4 g; Fat 4 g; Saturates 1 g

easy

15 mins

45 mins

(🍳) **COOK'S TIP**

Once the fish and vegetables are cooked, you could process the soup in a food processor or blender and pass it through a strainer to give a smooth fish soup.

As with many traditional French fish stews and soups, the fish and soup are served separately with a strongly flavored sauce passed around to accompany it.

# Bouillabaisse

1 To begin, make the red bell pepper and saffron sauce. Brush the red pepper quarters with a little of the olive oil. Place under a preheated hot broiler, cook for 5–6 minutes on each side until charred and tender. Remove from the heat and place in a plastic bag until cool enough to handle. Peel the skins away .

2 Place the bell pepper pieces into a food processor with the egg yolk, saffron, chili flakes, lemon juice, and seasoning and process until smooth. Begin adding the remaining olive oil, drop by drop, until the mixture begins to thicken. Continue adding the olive oil in a steady stream until it is all incorporated and the mixture is thick. Add a little hot water if it seems too thick.

3 In a large pan, heat the olive oil, add the onions, leek, garlic, and fennel and cook for 10–15 minutes until softened and starting to color. Add the tomatoes, thyme, orange rind, and seasoning and fry for a further 5 minutes until the tomatoes have collapsed.

4 Add the fish bouillon and bring to a boil. Simmer gently for 10 minutes until all the vegetables are tender. Add the fish and return to a boil. Simmer gently for 10 minutes until all the fish is tender.

5 When the soup is ready, toast the bread on both sides. Using a draining spoon, divide the fish between serving plates. Add some of the soup to moisten the stew and serve with the bread. Pass around the red bell pepper and saffron sauce to accompany. Serve the remaining soup separately.

**SERVES  6 – 8**

5 tbsp olive oil
2 large onions, chopped finely
1 leek, chopped finely
4 garlic cloves, crushed
½ small fennel bulb, chopped finely
5 ripe tomatoes, skinned and chopped
1 sprig of fresh thyme
2 strips orange rind
6½ cups hot fish bouillon
4 lb 8oz/2 kg mixed fish, such as tilapia, sea bass, bream, red mullet, cod, skate, chopped coarsely; soft shell crabs, raw shrimp, crayfish (shellfish left whole)
12–18 thick slices French bread
salt and pepper

*saffron sauce*

1 red bell pepper, seeded and quartered
⅔ cup light olive oil
1 egg yolk
large pinch of saffron
pinch chili flakes
lemon juice, to taste

**NUTRITION**
Calories *844*; Sugars *10 g*; Protein *69 g*; Carbohydrate *49 g*; Fat *43 g*; Saturates *6 g*

★★★     moderate

🕐     1 hr

🕐     45 mins

This is a rich and flavorful stew of slowly cooked squid, in a sauce of tomatoes and red wine. The squid becomes very tender.

# Squid Stew

**SERVES 4**

1 lb 10 oz/750 g squid
3 tbsp olive oil
1 onion, chopped
3 garlic cloves, chopped finely
1 tsp fresh thyme leaves
14 oz/400 g canned chopped tomatoes
2/3 cup red wine
1¼ cups water
1 tbsp chopped fresh parsley
salt and pepper

1 To prepare whole squid, hold the body firmly and grasp the tentacles just inside the body. Pull firmly to remove the innards. Find the transparent "quill" and remove. Grasp the wings on the outside of the body and pull to remove the outer skin. Trim the tentacles just below the beak and reserve. Wash the body and tentacles under cold running water. Slice the body into rings. Drain well on paper towels.

2 Heat the oil in a large, flameproof casserole. Add the prepared squid and cook over medium heat, stirring occasionally, until lightly browned.

3 Reduce the heat and add the onion, garlic, and thyme. Cook for another 5 minutes until softened.

4 Stir in the tomatoes, red wine, and water. Bring to a boil and cook in a preheated oven, 275°F/140°C, for 2 hours. Stir in the parsley and season to taste. Serve immediately.

**NUTRITION**
Calories 284; Sugars 5 g; Protein 31 g;
Carbohydrate 9 g; Fat 12 g; Saturates 2 g

easy
20 mins
2 hrs 15 mins

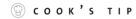 **COOK'S TIP**

This recipe can be used as the basis for a more substantial fish stew. Before adding the parsley, add extra seafood such as scallops, pieces of fish fillet, and large shrimp. Cook for another 2 minutes.

Fideua is a pasta dish which can be found south of Valencia, in western Spain. It is very like a paella, but is made with very fine pasta.

# Fideua

1 Heat the olive oil in a large, heavy skillet or paella pan. Add the onion and cook over low heat for 5 minutes until softened. Add the garlic and cook for another 30 seconds. Add the saffron and paprika and stir well. Add the tomatoes and cook for a further 2–3 minutes until they have collapsed.

2 Add the vermicelli and stir well. Add the wine and boil rapidly until it has been absorbed.

3 Add the fish bouillon, shrimp, mussels, squid, and clams. Stir and return to a low simmer for 10 minutes until the shrimp and squid are cooked through and the mussels and clams have opened. Discard any that remain shut. The bouillon should be almost completely absorbed.

4 Add the parsley and season to taste with salt and pepper. Serve immediately in warmed bowls, with lemon wedges.

SERVES 6

3 tbsp olive oil
1 large onion, chopped
2 garlic cloves, chopped finely
pinch of saffron, crushed
½ tsp paprika
3 tomatoes, peeled, seeded, and chopped
12 oz/350 g egg vermicelli, broken coarsely into 2-inch/5-cm lengths
⅔ cup white wine
1¼ cups fish bouillon
12 large raw shrimp
18 live mussels, scrubbed and bearded
12 oz/350 g cleaned squid, cut into rings
18 large clams, scrubbed
2 tbsp chopped fresh parsley
salt and pepper
lemon wedges, to serve

NUTRITION
Calories 373; Sugars 4 g; Protein 23 g; Carbohydrate 52 g; Fat 8 g; Saturates 1 g

 moderate

10 mins

20 mins

🍳 COOK'S TIP

Use whatever combination of shellfish you prefer. Try crayfish, shrimp, and angler fish.

Using curry paste in this recipe makes it quick and easy to prepare. It makes an ideal family supper.

# Coriander Cod Curry

### SERVES 4

1 tbsp vegetable oil

1 small onion, chopped

2 garlic cloves, chopped

1-inch/2.5-cm piece of fresh gingerroot, chopped coarsely

2 large ripe tomatoes, peeled and chopped coarsely

²⁄₃ cup fish bouillon

1 tbsp medium curry paste

1 tsp ground coriander

14 oz/400 g canned garbanzo beans, drained and rinsed

1 lb 10 oz/750 g cod fillet, cut into large chunks

4 tbsp chopped fresh cilantro

4 tbsp thick yogurt

salt and pepper

steamed basmati rice, to serve

1 Heat the oil in a large pan and add the onion, garlic, and ginger. Cook over low heat for 4–5 minutes until softened. Remove from the heat. Put the onion mixture into a food processor or blender with the tomatoes and fish bouillon and process until smooth.

2 Return to the pan with the curry paste, ground coriander, and garbanzo beans. Mix together well, then simmer gently for 15 minutes until thickened.

3 Add the pieces of fish and return to a simmer. Cook for 5 minutes until the fish is just tender. Remove from the heat and set aside for 2–3 minutes.

4 Stir in the cilantro and yogurt. Season and serve with basmati rice.

### NUTRITION

Calories *310*; Sugars *4 g*; Protein *42 g*; Carbohydrate *19 g*; Fat *8 g*; Saturates *1 g*

    easy

10 mins

25 mins

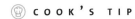 COOK'S TIP

Instead of cod, you can make this curry using raw shrimp and omitting the garbanzo beans.

Like all Thai curries, this one has as its base a paste of chiles and spices and a sauce of coconut milk.

# Red Shrimp Curry

1 Make the red curry paste. Put all the ingredients in a blender or spice grinder and blend to a smooth paste, adding a little water if necessary. Alternatively, pound the ingredients using a mortar and pestle until smooth. Set aside.

2 Heat the oil in a wok or skillet until almost smoking. Add the chopped garlic and fry until golden. Add 1 tablespoon of the curry paste and cook, stirring constantly, for a further minute. Add half the coconut milk, the fish sauce, and the sugar. Stir well until the mixture has thickened slightly.

3 Add the shrimp and simmer for 3–4 minutes until they turn color. Add the remaining coconut milk, the lime leaves, and fresh red chile. Cook for another 2–3 minutes until the shrimp are just tender.

4 Add the basil leaves and stir until wilted. Transfer to a warmed serving dish and serve immediately.

**SERVES 4**

2 tbsp vegetable oil
1 garlic clove, chopped finely
1 tbsp red curry paste (see below)
scant 1 cup coconut milk
2 tbsp Thai fish sauce
1 tsp sugar
12 large raw shrimp, deveined
2 kaffir lime leaves, shredded finely
1 small fresh red chile, deseeded and sliced thinly
10 leaves Thai basil, or ordinary basil

*red curry paste*
3 dried long red chiles
½ tsp ground coriander
¼ tsp ground cumin
½ tsp ground black pepper
2 garlic cloves, chopped
2 lemongrass stalks, chopped
1 kaffir lime leaf, chopped finely
1 tsp grated fresh gingerroot or galangal
1 tsp shrimp paste (optional)
½ tsp salt

**NUTRITION**
Calories *149*; Sugars *4 g*; Protein *15 g*; Carbohydrate *6 g*; Fat *7 g*; Saturates *1 g*

 easy

15 mins

 10 mins

A rich dish of layers of pasta, with seafood and mushrooms in a tomato sauce, topped with béchamel sauce and baked until golden.

# Seafood Lasagna

### SERVES 4

4 tbsp butter
6 tbsp flour
1 tsp mustard powder
2½ cups milk
2 tbsp olive oil
1 onion, chopped
2 garlic cloves, chopped finely
1 tbsp fresh thyme leaves
3 cups mixed mushrooms, sliced
⅔ cup white wine
14 oz/400 g canned chopped tomatoes
1 lb/450 g mixed skinless white fish fillets, cubed
8 oz/225 g fresh scallops, trimmed
4–6 sheets fresh lasagna
8 oz/225 g drained and chopped mozzarella cheese
salt and pepper

### NUTRITION

Calories 790; Sugars 23 g; Protein 55 g; Carbohydrate 74 g; Fat 32 g; Saturates 19 g

easy

30 mins

1 hr 20 mins

1 Melt the butter in a pan. Add the flour and mustard powder and stir until smooth. Simmer gently for 2 minutes without coloring. Gradually add the milk, whisking until smooth. Bring to a boil and simmer for 2 minutes. Remove from the heat and set aside. Cover the surface of the sauce with plastic wrap to prevent a skin from forming.

2 Heat the oil in a skillet and add the onion, garlic, and thyme. Cook gently for 5 minutes until softened. Add the mushrooms and fry for another 5 minutes until softened. Stir in the wine and boil rapidly until nearly evaporated. Stir in the tomatoes. Bring to a boil and simmer, covered, for 15 minutes. Season and set aside.

3 Grease a lasagna dish. Spoon half the tomato sauce in the dish and top with half the fish and scallops.

4 Layer half the lasagna over the fish, pour over half the white sauce, and add half the mozzarella. Repeat these layers, finishing with the white sauce and mozzarella.

5 Bake the lasagna in a preheated oven at 400°F/200°C for 35–40 minutes until the top is bubbling and golden and the fish is cooked through. Remove the dish from the oven and let it stand on a heat-resistant surface or mat for 10 minutes before serving.

You can use whatever combination of shellfish you like in this recipe—it is poached in a savoury bouillon and served with freshly cooked spaghetti.

# Seafood Spaghetti

1 Heat the oil in a large saucepan and fry the onion with the lemon juice, garlic, and celery for 3–4 minutes until just softened.

2 Pour in the bouillon and wine. Bring to a boil and add the tarragon and mussels. Cover and simmer for 5 minutes. Add the shrimp, squid and crab claws to the pan, mix together, and cook for 3–4 minutes until the mussels have opened, the shrimp are pink, and the squid is opaque. Discard the tarragon and any mussels that have not opened.

3 Meanwhile, cook the spaghetti in a saucepan of boiling water according to the instructions on the package. Drain well.

4 Add the spaghetti to the shellfish mixture and toss together. Season with salt and pepper to taste.

5 Transfer to warm serving plates and spoon over the cooking juices. Serve garnished with freshly chopped tarragon.

**SERVES 4**

2 tsp olive oil

1 small red onion, chopped finely

1 tbsp lemon juice

1 garlic clove, crushed

2 celery stalks, chopped finely

²⁄₃ cup fresh fish bouillon

²⁄₃ cup dry white wine

small bunch fresh tarragon

1 lb/450 g fresh mussels, prepared

225 g/8 oz fresh shrimp, peeled and deveined

8 oz/225 g baby squid, cleaned, trimmed, and sliced into rings

8 small cooked crab claws, cracked and peeled

8 oz/225 g spaghetti

salt and pepper

2 tbsp chopped fresh tarragon, to garnish

**NUTRITION**

Calories 372; Sugars 3 g; Protein 33 g; Carbohydrate 45 g; Fat 5 g; Saturates 1 g

easy

20 mins

30 mins

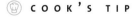 **COOK'S TIP**

Crab claws contain lean crab meat. Ask your fish store to crack the claws for you, leaving the pincers intact, because the shell is very tough.

This is an attractive dish to serve as an accompaniment, especially at parties, and will also freeze well.

# Shrimp *with* Spinach

### SERVES 4 – 6

8 oz/225 g frozen shrimp

12 oz/350 g canned spinach purée or frozen spinach, thawed and chopped

2 tomatoes

²⁄₃ cup oil

½ tsp mustard seeds

½ tsp onion seeds

1 tsp fresh gingerroot, chopped finely

1 tsp fresh garlic, crushed

1 tsp chili powder

1 tsp salt

1 Place the shrimp in a bowl of cold water and set aside to defrost thoroughly.

2 Drain the can of spinach purée, if using.

3 Using a sharp knife, cut the tomatoes into slices.

4 Heat the oil in a large skillet. Add the mustard and onion seeds to the pan.

5 Reduce the heat and add the tomatoes, spinach, gingerroot, garlic, chili powder, and salt to the pan and stir-fry for about 5–7 minutes.

6 Drain the shrimp thoroughly.

7 Add the shrimp to the spinach mixture in the pan. Gently stir the shrimp and spinach mixture until well combined, cover, and let simmer over low heat for about 7–10 minutes.

8 Transfer the shrimp and spinach to a serving dish and serve hot.

### NUTRITION

Calories *404*; Sugars *2 g*; Protein *13 g*; Carbohydrate *2 g*; Fat *39 g*; Saturates *5 g*

 easy

 30 mins

 20 mins

(🍳) COOK'S TIP

If using frozen spinach, it should be thawed and squeezed dry before using. You could use fresh spinach, if you prefer.

A *tagine* is an earthenware cooking dish that has a domed lid with a steam hole. This recipe can be made in an ordinary pan.

# Moroccan Fish Tagine

1 Heat the olive oil in a large pan or flameproof casserole. Add the onion and cook gently for 10 minutes, without allowing it to color, until softened. Add the saffron, cinnamon, coriander, cumin, and turmeric and cook for another 30 seconds, stirring.

2 Add the chopped tomatoes and fish bouillon and stir well. Bring to a boil, cover, and simmer for 15 minutes. Uncover and simmer for an additional 20–35 minutes until the sauce has thickened.

3 Cut each red mullet in half then add the pieces to the pan, pushing them into the sauce. Simmer gently for 5–6 minutes until the fish is just cooked.

4 Carefully stir in the olives, preserved lemon, and the cilantro. Season to taste and serve with couscous.

SERVES 4

2 tbsp olive oil
1 large onion, chopped finely
large pinch saffron strands
½ tsp ground cinnamon
1 tsp ground coriander
½ tsp ground cumin
½ tsp ground turmeric
7 oz/200 g canned chopped tomatoes
1¼ cups fish bouillon
4 small red mullet, cleaned, boned, and heads and tails removed
¼ cup pitted green olives
1 tbsp chopped preserved lemon
3 tbsp fresh chopped cilantro
salt and pepper
couscous, to serve

NUTRITION
Calories *188*; Sugars *5 g*; Protein *17 g*; Carbohydrate *7 g*; Fat *11 g*; Saturates *1 g*

 easy

10 mins

 1 hr 15 mins

 COOK'S TIP

To preserve lemons, take enough to fill a preserving jar. Quarter them lengthways without cutting right through. Pack with 2 oz/55 g sea salt per lemon. Add the juice of 1 more lemon and cover with water. Leave for 1 month

This is an impressive-looking Catalan dish using two classic Spanish cooking methods—the *sofrito* and the *picada*.

# Spanish Fish Stew

**SERVES 4**

5 tbsp olive oil
2 large onions, chopped finely
2 tomatoes, peeled, seeded, and diced
2 slices white bread, crusts removed
4 almonds, toasted
3 garlic cloves, chopped coarsely
12 oz/350 g cooked lobster
7 oz/200 g cleaned squid
7 oz/200 g angler fish fillet
7 oz/200 g cod fillet, skinned
1 tbsp all-purpose flour
6 large raw shrimp
6 crayfish
18 live mussels, scrubbed, beards removed
8 large live clams, scrubbed
1 tbsp chopped fresh parsley
½ cup brandy
salt and pepper

**NUTRITION**
Calories 346; Sugars 4 g; Protein 37 g;
Carbohydrate 11 g; Fat 13 g; Saturates 2 g

 challenging

30 mins

1 hr

1 Heat 3 tablespoons of the oil and cook the onions gently for 10–15 minutes until lightly golden. Add the tomatoes and cook until they have softened.

2 Heat 1 tablespoon of the remaining oil and cook the slices of bread until crisp. Break into pieces and put into a mortar with the almonds and 2 garlic cloves. Pound to a fine paste. Alternatively, process in a food processor.

3 Split the lobster lengthwise. Remove and discard the intestinal vein, the stomach sac, and the spongy gills. Crack the claws and remove the meat. Take out the flesh from the tail and chop into large chunks. Slice the squid into rings.

4 Season the angler fish, cod, and lobster and dust with flour. Heat a little of the remaining oil and separately brown the angler fish, cod, lobster, squid, shrimp, and crayfish. Arrange them in a flameproof casserole as they brown.

5 Add the mussels and clams and the remaining garlic and parsley. Set the pan over low heat. Pour over the brandy and ignite. When the flames have died down, add the tomato mixture and just enough water to cover. Bring to a boil and simmer for 3–4 minutes until the mussels and clams have opened. Stir in the bread mixture and season. Simmer for another 5 minutes and serve.

Based on a traditional Cuban recipe, this dish is similar to Spanish paella, but it has the added kick of dark rum.

# Fish *and* Rice *with* Dark Rum

1 Place the cubes of fish in a bowl and add the cumin, oregano, lime juice, rum, and sugar. Season to taste with salt and pepper. Mix thoroughly, cover with plastic wrap, and set aside to chill for 2 hours.

2 Meanwhile, place the garlic, onion, and bell peppers in a large pan. Pour in the bouillon and stir in the rice. Bring to a boil, lower the heat, cover, and simmer for 15 minutes.

3 Gently stir in the fish and the marinade juices. Bring back to a boil and simmer, uncovered, stirring occasionally but taking care not to break up the fish, for about 10 minutes until the fish is cooked and the rice is tender.

4 Season with salt and pepper and transfer to a warmed serving plate. Garnish with fresh oregano and lime wedges and serve with crusty bread.

**SERVES 4**

1 lb/450 g firm white fish fillets (such as cod or angler fish), skinned and cut into 1-inch/2.5-cm cubes
2 tsp ground cumin
2 tsp dried oregano
2 tbsp lime juice
2/3 cup dark rum
1 tbsp molasses sugar
3 garlic cloves, chopped finely
1 large onion, chopped
1 each medium red bell pepper, green bell pepper, and yellow bell pepper, seeded and sliced into rings
5 cups fish bouillon
1¾ cups long-grain rice
salt and pepper
crusty bread, to serve

*to garnish*
fresh oregano leaves
lime wedges

**NUTRITION**
Calories *547*; Sugars *9 g*; Protein *27 g*; Carbohydrate *85 g*; Fat *4 g*; Saturates *1 g*

moderate

35 mins

2 hrs 15 mins

A different way to make the most of crab, this rich-tasting and colorful risotto is full of interesting flavors.

# Crab Risotto

**SERVES 4 – 6**

2–3 large red bell peppers
3 tbsp olive oil
1 onion, chopped finely
1 small fennel bulb, chopped finely
2 celery stalks, chopped finely
$\frac{1}{4}$–$\frac{1}{2}$ tsp cayenne pepper
3 cups risotto rice
1 lb 12 oz/800 g canned Italian peeled plum
   tomatoes, drained and chopped
$\frac{1}{4}$ cup dry white vermouth (optional)
$6\frac{3}{4}$ cups fish or chicken bouillon, simmering
1 lb/450 g fresh cooked crab meat
$\frac{1}{4}$ cup lemon juice
2–4 tbsp chopped fresh parsley or chervil
salt and pepper

1 Broil the bell peppers until the skins are charred. Transfer to a plastic bag and twist to seal. When cool enough to handle, peel off the charred skins, working over a bowl to catch the juices. Remove the cores and seeds. Chop the flesh and set aside, reserving the juices.

2 Heat the olive oil in a large heavy-based pan. Add the onion, fennel, and celery and cook over low heat, stirring occasionally, for 2–3 minutes until the vegetables are softened. Add the cayenne and rice and cook, stirring frequently, for about 2 minutes until the rice is translucent and well coated.

3 Stir in the chopped tomatoes and vermouth, if using. The liquid will bubble and steam rapidly. When the liquid is almost absorbed, add a ladleful (about 1 cup) of the simmering bouillon. Cook, stirring constantly, until the liquid is completely absorbed.

4 Continue adding the bouillon, about half a cup at a time, allowing each addition to be absorbed before adding the next. This should take 20–25 minutes. The risotto should have a creamy consistency and the rice should be tender, but still firm to the bite.

5 Stir in the red bell peppers and reserved juices, the crab meat, lemon juice, and parsley or chervil and heat. Season with salt and pepper to taste. Serve the risotto immediately.

**NUTRITION**
Calories *447*; Sugars *11 g*; Protein *22 g*;
Carbohydrate *62 g*; Fat *13 g*; Saturates *2 g*

 moderate

15 mins

50 mins

Although lobster is expensive, this dish is worth it. Keeping it simple lets the lobster flavor come through.

# Rich Lobster Risotto

1 Heat the oil and half the butter in a large heavy pan over medium heat. Add the shallots and cook, stirring occasionally, for about 2 minutes until just beginning to soften. Add the rice and cayenne and cook, stirring frequently, for about 2 minutes until the rice is translucent and well coated with the oil and butter.

2 Pour in the vermouth: it will bubble and steam rapidly and evaporate almost immediately. Add a ladleful (about 1 cup) of the simmering bouillon and cook, stirring constantly, until the bouillon is completely absorbed.

3 Continue adding the bouillon, about half a cup at a time, letting each addition be completely absorbed before adding the next—never allow the rice to cook "dry." This process should take about 20–25 minutes. The risotto should have a creamy consistency and the rice should be tender, but still firm to the bite.

4 Stir in the tomatoes and cream and cook for about 2 minutes.

5 Add the cooked lobster meat with the remaining butter and chervil and cook long enough to just heat the lobster meat gently. Serve immediately.

**SERVES 4**

1 tbsp vegetable oil
4 tbsp sweet butter
2 shallots, chopped finely
$2\frac{2}{3}$ cups risotto rice
$\frac{1}{2}$ tsp cayenne pepper
5 tbsp dry white vermouth
$6\frac{1}{4}$ cups shellfish, fish, or chicken bouillon, simmering
16 cherry tomatoes, quartered and seeded
2–3 tbsp heavy or whipping cream
1 lb/450 g cooked lobster meat, cut into coarse chunks
2 tbsp chopped fresh chervil or dill
salt and white pepper

**NUTRITION**
Calories *688*; Sugars *3 g*; Protein *32 g*; Carbohydrate *69 g*; Fat *31 g*; Saturates *16 g*

 moderate

 10 mins

25 mins

Here, fresh sardines are baked with eggs, herbs, and vegetables to form a dish similar to an omelet.

# Fresh Baked Sardines

**SERVES 4**

2 tbsp olive oil
2 large onions, sliced into rings
3 garlic cloves, chopped
2 large zucchini, cut into sticks
3 tbsp fresh thyme, stalks removed
8 large sardine fillets
1 cup grated Parmesan cheese
4 eggs, beaten
²⁄₃ cup milk
salt and pepper

1 Heat 1 tablespoon of the olive oil in a skillet. Add the onion rings and chopped garlic and fry over a low heat, stirring occasionally, for 2–3 minutes.

2 Add the zucchini to the skillet and cook, stirring occasionally, for about 5 minutes or until golden. Stir in 2 tablespoons of the thyme.

3 Place half the onions and zucchini in the base of a large ovenproof dish. Top with the sardine fillets and half the grated Parmesan cheese.

4 Place the remaining onions and zucchini on top and sprinkle with the remaining thyme.

5 Combine the eggs and milk in a bowl and season to taste with salt and pepper. Pour the mixture over the vegetables and sardines in the dish. Sprinkle the remaining Parmesan cheese over the top.

6 Bake in a preheated oven, 350°F/ 180°C, for 20–25 minutes or until golden and set. Serve immediately.

**NUTRITION**
Calories *690*; Sugars *12 g*; Protein *63 g*;
Carbohydrate *17 g*; Fat *42 g*; Saturates *15 g*

 challenging

35 mins

20–25 mins

🖐 **COOK'S TIP**

If you cannot find sardines that are large enough to fillet, use small mackerel instead.

This is a dramatic-looking dish owing to the inclusion of the cuttlefish ink. Although typically Spanish, here it is teamed with polenta .

# Cuttlefish *in their own* Ink

1 Cut off the cuttlefish tentacles in front of the eyes and remove the beak from the center of the tentacles. Cut the head from the body and discard. Cut open the body section along the dark colored back. Remove the cuttle bone and the entrails, reserving the ink sac. Skin the body. Chop the flesh roughly and set aside. Split open the ink sac and dilute the ink in a little water. Set aside.

2 Heat the oil in a large pan and add the onion. Cook gently for 8–10 minutes until softened and golden. Add the garlic and cook for another 30 seconds. Add the cuttlefish and cook for another 5 minutes until starting to brown. Add the paprika and stir for 30 seconds before adding the tomatoes. Cook for 2–3 minutes until collapsed.

3 Add the red wine, fish bouillon, and diluted ink and stir well. Bring to a boil and simmer gently, uncovered, for 25 minutes until the cuttlefish is tender and the sauce has thickened. Season to taste with salt and pepper.

4 Meanwhile, cook the polenta according to the package instructions. When cooked, remove from the heat and stir in the parsley and seasoning.

5 Divide the polenta among plates and top with the cuttlefish and its sauce.

SERVES 4

1 lb/450 g small cuttlefish or squid, with their ink sacs
4 tbsp olive oil
1 small onion, chopped finely
2 garlic cloves, chopped finely
1 tsp paprika
2 ripe medium tomatoes, peeled, seeded, and chopped
$2/3$ cup red wine
$2/3$ cup fish bouillon
$1^2/3$ cups instant polenta
3 tbsp chopped fresh flatleaf parsley
salt and pepper

NUTRITION
Calories *430*; Sugars *2 g*; Protein *24 g*; Carbohydrate *44 g*; Fat *14 g*; Saturates *2 g*

 challenging

15 mins

 45 mins

# Index